MONEY AND MANIFESTING

By

Dyan Garris

D1089621

MONEY AND MANIFESTING

Dyan Garris

www.voiceoftheangels.com
www.dyangarris.com

Journeymakers, Inc.

Published in the United States of America.
No part of this book may be used or
reproduced in any manner whatsoever
without the written permission of the publisher.

Fourth printing: May 2008.

Cover art by Limebar Creative

ISBN: 978-0-9776140-6-6

Printed in the United States of America
10 9 8 7 6 5 4 3 2 1

The Real Secret of Manifesting

It is not enough to think positively, repeat affirmations, and attract positive energy. We must implement and integrate this learning into our daily lives. This is the real secret of manifesting.

Foreword

People tell me that I'm lucky, that I'm blessed. Such statements diminish the ability we have to imagine and achieve our own success. It is as if good fortune is handed out—or not—by an outside source.

I do believe that the good Lord watches over me. But I also realize my part in the journey. I envision what I want, recognize the many ways it may be attained, keep my eyes open for helpful people and choices along the way, and invest the time and effort required. Throughout it all, I trust that it all will work out favorably. I have no doubt that I will succeed.

Dyan Garris' book, *Money and Manifesting,* tells how you also can be successful and acquire the wealth you desire. She offers examples and specific guidelines on how this can be done. Like all things worthwhile, you may have to work at some of the steps before you can do them with ease. But why not go ahead and try? You have so much to gain.

Marshall Brodien
Magician and Creator of TV Magic Cards

CONTENTS

Nicholas Fortuna...1

What's Wrong With Positive Thinking?.............7

The Root Chakra 10

Why Positive Thoughts and Passion Are
    Not Enough... 12

The Other Chakras and The Law of
    Attraction 13

Success – The Measure of Success 14

Carla 17

Barriers to Manifesting – Patterns,
    Belief Systems, and Illusions...................... 23

Poverty Consciousness 23

Fear... 24

Duality Consciousness..................................... 27

Karma 28

Entitlement 29

The Illusion of Separation............................... 31

The Illusion of Limitation 33

Fifteen Million Dollars.................................... 37

Illusions of the Linear Mind – Perceptions....... 39

The Khaki Shorts... 39

Person A & Person B 41

The Illusion of Time 43

Lucky.. 45

Chakra Balance and Stuck Energy 51

The First Chakra 53

The Second Chakra 55

The Third Chakra.. 58

The Fourth Chakra.. 61

The Fifth Chakra 63

The Sixth Chakra 65

The Seventh Chakra 67

Yantras and Mantras 69

Elayne 77

Chakra Balancing – Part I 85

Breathing & Relaxation Techniques 87

Prana Breathing 88

Grounding... 89

Centering 90

Create a Sanctuary.. 92

Nicholas 97

Chakra Balancing – Part II 101

Carlos.. 105

Patterns, Habits, Change and the Mind, Body,
    Spirit Team.. 107

The Integration of Mind, Body, and Spirit...... 112

Bobby.. 117

Money as Energy – Breaking Down the
    Barriers to Manifesting............................. 123

The Feng Shui Money Tree – Something Out
    of Nothing... 127

Lucky 131

Working with the Energy of Money 135

Debt and Financial Responsibility 137

Lucky 141

Manifesting 101... 143

Responsibility and Choices............................. 145

Lucky and Nicholas.. 147

Green Lights... 149

The Basic Principles of Manifesting................ 151

Detach... 152

Don't Give Up – Let Go and Release 153

Lucky 157

Carla 159

Being Grateful 165
Judgments 166
Forgiveness 167
Carla 169
Epilogue 173

Introduction

The very first thing to understand about money is that we do not "make" money. We create and open pathways to the flow of the energy of money. Money is energy. In and of itself it has no power. The power it has is our perception that it has power and this is what fuels the energy of money. These perceptions stem from illusion, perspectives, and deep seated belief systems.

If we understand these concepts as a basis, then we can begin to understand that we need to learn to open pathways of energy flow. Part of that process is learning how energy works, how we can utilize that energy, and subsequently learn to manifest.

What makes this book different is that you will learn how to actually transform energy and learn how to integrate energy and align the mind, body, and spirit so that the things you are manifesting can actually occur. This is called synchronicity.

The magic of synchronicity can't happen if your will isn't aligned with universal will because we cannot manifest from a place of ego, which is the place of wants, needs, and desires. This is the place where the mind decides what it wants irrespective of what the spirit came to do.

And synchronicity can't happen if you don't integrate and implement the learning. Reading about how to manifest is one thing. Thinking positive thoughts is another thing. But actually implementing, and clearing a pathway for the energy to travel on and then integrating, is quite another matter.

The energy of money resides in the root chakra. In order to manifest anything we need to understand the chakra system, why it's a factor, and learn how to balance and clear our chakras and chakra system. You will learn how to do that here as well. It is not difficult. But it is integral to the process of manifesting anything.

And we will be breaking down the illusion of money as it relates to self worth. Money as we know it is basically pieces of paper. Those that have learned to equate their intrinsic value and ultimate "success" with money should seriously consider when they became pieces of paper.

These illusions and perspectives have to do with learned patterns and belief systems; and here you will learn about these things, where they originated from and what to do about them too.

We will go beyond positive thinking and "you are what you attract" and "you are what you think about." While those things are certainly true, just knowing about those or engaging in positive thinking doesn't take you to the next steps.

Positive thinking and affirmations do not necessarily lead you to learning how to actually create money flow in your life. You have to integrate the positive thoughts into your belief system as truth. They have to take true form in the chakra system and replace the old patterns. This is what we can then build a foundation on, and subsequently an amazing new house.

You will learn how to integrate the energy of mind, body, and spirit and thus be able to attract and create anything you choose, not just money.

I wrote the book the way I did for a reason. That is so that while you're reading it you're engaging left brain, right brain, and the different chakras as well. The book itself is an exercise in integration. And the characters each have blocks to manifesting. In one way or another they are each in their own way of getting what they want.

Everything is a reflection; and if you can see yourself reflected here even in one small aspect, you will then have the keys to unlocking the doors to manifesting. All it takes is the knowledge of how to connect the dots, the ability to turn the key in the lock, and the willingness to step through the doors.

*Synchronicity is what happens when the
mind, body, and spirit are working together
as a team.*

*Manifesting is bringing all layers of the
etheric body, mind, physical body, and spirit
together in synchronicity.*

Value and worth are perceptions.

Nicholas Fortuna

Nicholas shook off the night and the mild hangover like a slightly used and rumpled towel thrown carelessly on the granite floor of his bedroom. The ambient glow of the LED lighting embedded into the thick slab softly lit the way to the bathroom. Warm and toasty heat rose up like a sweet good morning kiss to gently greet his feet. He turned the knob on the handcast gold and jewel encrusted sink and watched, fascinated, as the water gently bubbled up like a flowing fountain. He splashed some cool water on the chiseled face that was God's gift to everyone.

Actually, he didn't believe in God. He believed in things he could see and feel and taste and touch. He believed in himself. He believed in the power of money. He believed in the power of his fame. It all proved beyond any doubt that everyone, *everyone* loved him. It proved that he was indeed a rare jewel in a sea of fool's gold.

He gave his washboard abs of steel a little jab with one long finger as he flashed himself a brilliant, high voltage smile. His reflection in the mirror responded in kind. Yes, those abs and teeth were perfect along with everything else. He grinned again in delight and Adonis grinned back at him.

Pushing a small button in a control panel hidden in the mirror brought his personal maid scurrying in with a steaming, frothy cup of rare Panamanian coffee that he'd been lucky enough to win at auction.

With heavily lidded and downcast eyes, a shy and somewhat plump Juanita handed him the warm cup. As he took a sip he made a mental note to fire her. It was the first time he'd really looked at her. She wasn't particularly easy on the eyes; and she'd forgotten to put a shot or two of his favorite exotic liquor, Arrack, in it. He wanted to be surrounded by beauty and competence at all times. She'd have to go. *Today.*

He savored the joy and power of his immense wealth just as much as the rare brew as he made his way through the French doors to the back yard and stuck one perfect toe into the sparkling, crystal clear pool. Heavenly.

The deep tropical pool wrapped around his oceanfront estate like a protective moat. He finished his exquisite but virgin java, set the platinum rimmed cup down, and entered the silky water which caressed his hard naked body like a soft cocoon. Later he would take a sauna, lift some weights, get dressed and go for a drive in his Jaguar or Ferrari, maybe even get a bite to eat. He took great pleasure in outsmarting and eluding the paparazzi and sometimes he just liked to be out among the common people. It gave them a thrill.

Nicholas was rich beyond rich. He was also famous. He had known he was destined for this greatness when he was twelve years old. He had thought of nothing else since his scumbag, drug addicted father had run away like a rabbit after his mother died of an accidental overdose. Nicholas was shuffled around and told what to do by so many people after that he lost count. It made his head spin. None of the relatives wanted to take him in because of how much it would ultimately cost them. Apparently another mouth to feed meant he wasn't a very valuable commodity. He was worth less than a shovelful of dirt. *Worthless.* He got the message loud and clear.

He ended up in the foster care system and never was able to stay too long in one place. That was fine with him because most of the foster care parents were just as messed up as his own had been. All they really wanted was the money the state paid them to take him in. Money was what mattered.

He determined then that he would never feel like a powerless pawn in someone else's game ever again. Never. He would become rich and famous someday. No one would be able to tell him what to do, where to go, or how to live his life. No one would ever be able to pull the rug out from under him again. He put every ounce of his youthful energy and every waking moment on it. Yes, someday he would be the one in charge of rug pulling.

Through the crazy confusion of that time period, he eventually discovered that his mother had left him a great gift. Those hypnotic navy blue eyes he had inherited from her worked their manipulative magic on anyone he chose. He discovered he could charm and mesmerize a cardboard box if he wanted to.

Along with the knowledge of that power came also the surprising and delightful ability to morph into any character he wanted to be. He practiced this until he had honed the skill into a very fine, sharp point. He definitely wanted to be anyone else but himself. This skill was what would later make him into the great, talented, and extremely well compensated actor that he now was. He loved his mother.

He still shuddered when he thought of the things he'd had to do to get here, though. He preferred not to think about them. Some things were just better off being left in the filthy dust of the past. And those days were long gone, just like Carolyn, who had left abruptly like a thief in the night taking everything with her including what was left of his heart. Yes, these things were better off not thought of because if he ever came across Carolyn again he would kill her.

The past didn't really matter. He was Nicholas Fortuna for *crissake*. He was powerful beyond powerful. He had more money than anyone could imagine. He was in charge and he had perfect control at all times.

5

What's Wrong With Positive Thinking?

Money. We all need it. We all want it. Or at least we think we do. Our society functions on this illusion. But the truth is that money is simply used as an accepted form of exchange. This could just as easily be something else. In economic terms it could be guns or butter or even beads. It doesn't matter. We believe that these pieces of paper that are our accepted form of exchange have value and so they do. We believe it with every fiber of our being. There is no doubt in our minds. And so it is. Money has perceived value and perceived power.

What we believe – our underlying belief systems – is really what has power. It is helpful to try to begin to see how our thoughts and beliefs shape the fabric of our lives. Whatever you believe begins to make a framework and foundation for your entire life. It's what you build on.

You're reading this book because you want to learn to take things a step further than just thinking positively. To do that you need to learn to integrate the functions of the mind, body, and spirit. And you need to get to the root of the matter and the core issues of whatever stands in your way of manifesting exactly what you desire.

You need to learn how thoughts become part of your belief system. Yes we create with our thoughts. Yes we attract what we create with our minds/thoughts. The power of positive thinking is not to be negated, but in and of itself it isn't enough. And we don't learn to integrate anything by just simply thinking positively.

Thoughts are coming from only one chakra. In order to manifest effectively, one must engage the power of all their chakras. One must clear a pathway so that the energy of all the chakras can flow and function together.

For example, let's say you sit there and think all kinds of positive thoughts. You try your hardest to attract money. Nothing happens and you wonder what is wrong. Here is part of what's wrong and we will explore the rest of why this hasn't worked for you a bit later: Somewhere in your belief system you don't believe it. You are in your own way. All of the positive thoughts in the world can't change anything if you don't integrate them as truth into your system. And in order to manifest they must resonate as truth in your root chakra first because *that is where the energy of creation exists.*

To begin, one needs to study exactly where these ingrained patterns and belief systems originated. We first learn our belief systems regarding money from our tribe, from our family. Their pattern becomes our pattern. Often, this is exactly what is in your way of manifesting because some of these belief systems are built on foundations of belief in fear, lack, self-loathing, and powerlessness. If you can first identify the patterns, you can change them.

Your relationship with money begins with a learned pattern that wasn't your own to begin with, and that pattern filters down and begins to resonate as truth in your own system.

Now in the alternative, let's say you sit there and think all kinds of positive thoughts and you do attract money. That's great! At some point, depending upon your learned pattern and belief systems, you may find yourself without it again. For example, someone might come along and swindle you, or you gamble it away, or you give it away, lose it all for "love," or in some other similar manner. We've all heard the incredible stories of multi-million dollar lottery winners who are penniless in a few years, or the child stars who made a fortune and then lost it by the time they were adults. These things seem unbelievable, but they happen because the core issues of the root chakra have not been healed.

The Root Chakra

For purposes of manifesting, it is important to understand exactly what energy resides in the root chakra because the energy of money resides there. The energy of sex, the energy of addiction, abuse, self-abuse, the rhythms of tribe, family, and group belief systems all reside there as well.

And great power resides in the root chakra. But it is the power that makes energy rise. It is the raw power to fuel transformation.

Where we get stuck and blocked is in the illusion of power and the belief that the things that simply reside there have power in and of themselves. They don't. The mind fools the body into believing the illusion. And the spirit keeps tugging at the mind and body in an effort of remembrance. However, there is power there; and you can access it freely and to your benefit if you understand it.

I'm talking about the power to make something out of nothing. The power to take the energy that resides in the root chakra and make it do something, make it work for you rather than against you. The goal is to make it rise up, rather than reach out in a parallel direction hoping to find self-validation. Then you can integrate this energy with the rest of the system to go up and out so it can return to you.

Anyone that has procreated a child has experienced the power of this chakra. Anyone that has meditated as a practice for long enough has experienced this "kundalini rising." Anyone that has used their physical body as an instrument of the expression of the love of their spirit has experienced this phenomenon.

11

Why Positive Thoughts and Passion Are Not Enough

When you're thinking positive thoughts and trying to create from your mind, you are using one chakra; and it isn't the root chakra, it's the sixth chakra. To have thoughts manifest on the earth plane, you have to connect up the energy of the root with the energy of the linear mind.

Think of yourself as a flower or plant. The root system is what feeds the rest of the organism. Water and nutrients are absorbed from the root; and the energy pushes the plant through the earth and up so that it grows, soaks up the sunlight, and eventually blooms, opens, and flowers.

Often it is said that one must do what they're passionate about and then the money will follow. But that is not necessarily true as many people have found out. Let's say you take that advice, you do what you're really, truly passionate about, and the following year you find yourself on the threshold of bankruptcy wondering what happened and cursing the powers that be.

It isn't enough to do your passion because passion comes from one chakra, the heart. You must figure out and repair your relationship with money at a basic and core level, at the root first. And then open a clear pathway for the two to be able to work together in harmony. This is key. It is more than just acting as if you have already received. This means giving up your illusions, patterns, and previous belief systems and opening up your mind, body, and spirit to infinite possibilities.

The Other Chakras and the Law of Attraction

The other chakras play a role in manifesting money as well. When you're learning to think positively and attract what you want into your life, you're first going to attract energy into and within an already existing framework. You can learn to attract what you're thinking about with some degree of success, but it will then filter through the chakra system and then through the perceptions that are already ingrained. So wherever you're blocked is where you're going to have challenges on the road to material wealth or anything else you're attempting to manifest.

By learning to clear and balance your chakras and function as an integrated and complete and whole person, you are opening a pipeline and corridor along which energy flows. And having that corridor open and clear and connected is how you begin to manifest the energy of money into your life. It's how you begin to manifest anything into your life.

Success – The Measure of Success

We are taught from a very young age to measure everything. Someone handed us an invisible yardstick and we've carried it around for years measuring and measuring.

We measure our height and weight and waistlines. We measure our growth and our progress with someone else's idea of milestones. We measure our food and our food ingredients because we are afraid to use our intuition. Some are even afraid of nourishment.

14

We measure our IQs. We measure our bank accounts. We measure ourselves against others. For years the size of one's car was an accepted measure of one's supposed success.

Lately, we use the quantity of the things that we have as a measure of success. We must be okay if we have three cars in the garage, two or three houses, a 401(k), stock options, and whatever else passes as someone's illusion of how success is supposed to show up.

Just exactly when did we become pieces of paper, inches, centimeters, teaspoons, and 1/4 cups?

When we expect and desire "success" to return to us as pieces of paper, this is what we are manifesting; and eventually, if we put enough energy on it, it will return to us that way.

Pieces of paper in and of themselves are completely worthless. It is the energy we put behind them that gives them the power they have today. It is an illusion.

It is the under-"lying" belief systems that shape perception.

If we insist upon "success" showing up and returning to us as money or things, we then limit the universe's ability to bring us what we need in other ways. We limit ourselves to our version of the story. In our attempts to be so big, have we really become so small?

The true measure of a man is not found in his wallet but in his heart. The only thing that is real is love. It's what everyone goes out of here saying, thinking about, and remembering.

Everything else is an illusion. So, how successful are you?

Carla

Curled up on the window seat like a lazy *gato* in the sun, Carla gazed out with almond shaped amber eyes at the panoramic view from the very attractive house she and her husband Carlos lived in.

Her English wasn't so great. Sometimes she got things a little mixed up. Looking out onto the peaceful park, she felt that the world was her clamshell now and here in America she would find her pearl.

The view of the park was as idyllic as something out of a masterpiece painted by Renoir or Monet. She could almost smell the bright, colorful, and pastel flowers through the window.

Carla considered herself a rather humble and uncomplicated person. She believed in simple things. She knew about karma and she knew what goes around comes around. And she also knew that she, Carla, was a very good person despite what others may think.

Her classic good looks and natural aura of aristocracy belied her poverty-stricken upbringing in Multuvia. She was determined that no one here would ever find out about her past. Living in this house made her feel wealthy and successful beyond her dreams. In fact, she felt like a real princess and free to create anything she wanted.

And she didn't want much. Since she was not a greedy person, certainly the universe would shine its sunbeams of abundance and prosperity upon her realm.

All she really wanted was a little store, selling metaphysical things like tarot cards. Certainly this was not too much to ask of the powers that were in charge of things?

She would dream about this every single day and someday this dream would become reality. She just knew it! She, Carla, had the gift of intuition. And her tarot cards had never been wrong. Not ever.

The universe had already been unbelievably kind to her by giving her this wonderful husband, Carlos, and the opportunity to come to America, become a citizen, and fulfill her dreams. As the sunshine filtering in from the window poured its warm and lovely magnificence upon her, she knew she had arrived.

Carlos had been married when she met him; but they had fallen wildly, passionately and madly in love. And love was always good, wasn't it?

The fates had conspired together to make this happen. She had seen it in her tarot cards before it ever happened. The cards were very powerful. They predicted it.

They had met when she had befriended his wife. At the time Carla had no money and no home and was living in the streets and under bridges, in camps, and in tents. She was a Multuvian gypsy and had been taught survival in a nomadic existence; but she knew she was destined for bigger and better things. The cards said so.

All she had at the time were the raggedy, tattered clothes on her back and her precious tarot cards. She never went anywhere without them. She had seen all

19

of the gorgeous and fine fashions in the window of her favorite store. In her mind's eye she saw herself wearing these very beautiful things someday. She never let go of that. It was as real to her as the ground she slept on.

In the afternoons as part of her daily wanderings, she would hover quietly in the shadows near the store to observe, imagine, and dream.

One day she saw a woman get out of an expensive looking automobile, go into the shop, and come out with many packages of the beautiful clothes.

Carla pushed aside a large pang of jealousy, gathered all of her courage, and approached the woman from her place in the murky shadows. She offered a tarot reading to the woman in exchange for a meal.

The startled woman looked down at Carla's slight frame and dark, wild and tangled hair with a mixture of surprise, compassion, and pity in her big, round, chocolate colored eyes. Carla gritted her teeth in silent resolve and determined in that moment that no one would ever look at her like that again.

To Carla's amazement, after a slight moment of hesitation, the lady agreed. She and the woman, Yolanda, went across the street to a small and cozy café. Carla, as promised, performed her particular brand of magic with her tarot cards in exchange for the first hot meal she'd had in months. She'd ordered pancakes and she could still taste their buttery richness, even now.

Afterward, Yolanda thanked her and, being the kind and sympathetic soul that she was, offered Carla some work around her house. There was something intriguing about this girl and Yolanda felt as if they already knew each other. She could use a maid to clean the house and do some yard work. Her husband was a successful *abogado*, after all; and she deserved to have a servant. In her opinion such a thing went hand in hand with success.

And that was how Carla came to scrub the toilets and floors and clean the dirty laundry of the Ortega family.

The attraction between Carlos and her had been instantaneous and electric. It was as if they had known each other forever. When it could be contained no longer, they had joined together like unbridled lightening in wild and explosive passion one evening while Yolanda was out playing cards with her friends and bragging about being able to afford a maid.

The gods and goddesses in charge of such things continued to shower them with sweet nectar from the heavens and weave their prolific love spell upon them.

She didn't care what anyone thought. Carlos belonged to her. She could feel it. She *knew* it and the cards even said so! They were meant to be together!

Eventually she and Carlos had run off together to America to start a new life, he leaving one child and that lazy cow of a soon to be ex-wife behind. What else could they do? It was *destino*.

The little cry from her own most beautiful child in the next room startled her suddenly out of her reverie. She must attend.

22

Barriers to Manifesting – Patterns, Belief Systems, and Illusions

Poverty Consciousness

You get invited to a picnic and are asked to bring something. You decide you will bring a sandwich. As you prepare the sandwich, your poverty consciousness (that is the consciousness that tells you that you don't have enough) kicks in and you decide that you can only afford to bring one half of a sandwich. So that is what you do.

On the way there you eat half of the sandwich yourself because you feel entitled to do so. When you get there no one wants to share it with you. You tell yourself that your sandwich must somehow be inferior, all the while thinking to yourself that you made it with good intentions. You do not understand what the problem is.

While you are talking about yourself to someone, the sandwich falls to the ground and ants become interested in it. You tell yourself that this sort of thing always happens to you and you do not know why.

What you are missing is that if you were paying attention, if you were not so self focused, if you covered the sandwich or made sure it was in a place where it wouldn't fall carelessly to the ground, you would still have it and be able to enjoy it or share its enjoyment with others, even though it is only one half of what it could be. This is self-sabotage.

It is also poverty consciousness. It is the belief in lack, the belief that there isn't enough, and the belief that one is completely unworthy of receiving.

Fear

A mindset and belief in poverty consciousness has an underlying foundation of fear. Fear blocks love. Fear blocks your attempts at manifesting. It does you no good to think positive thoughts if underneath it all you still believe in lack.

In this case you are in your own way. You must figure out when you first learned to resonate with this fear, where it is stuck, why it is stuck. Then you must clear it out of your energy field so that it no longer seems like truth to you.

Fear resides in the root chakra and makes its way up because the natural consciousness of the root chakra is "energy rising." Fear rises like a coiled snake as the energy that resides intrinsically in the base chakra begins to "take root." When the energy makes its way up to the sixth chakra the mind begins to accept this fearful energy as truth. But it's not. It's an illusion.

Our relationship with money is learned; and it is learned first from our family, our tribe, and our peers. This is where we first learn, take on as our own, and begin to implement the patterns of poverty consciousness and duality consciousness and money as a definition of self-worth.

We certainly aren't born with any knowledge of money and its role as an exchange or its attendant distortions. This we are taught. If you were brought up in an environment where money was an issue, i.e., there never seemed to be enough, you were treated as an unwanted intruder; or if you were taught that money was power, and safety, you have a distorted relationship with money. And if you were told that money defines who you are, you have a distorted relationship with money. There is nothing to be afraid of unless you truly believe that money itself has dominion.

Are you afraid of losing all your money? Are you afraid of having no money? Where did these fears originate from? If you had been born in a different time, not so long ago, you wouldn't have been afraid of these things – they would have been a natural way of life. It is illusion and learned perception that you need things and money to survive. Money and possessions are nice to have, but you don't *need* them to survive. You've just convinced yourself that you do. And this is what resonates as truth.

If you're willing to let go of that illusion and realize the truth that you can create anything you want, including the flow of money, there is nothing to be afraid of.

There is no success and there is no failure. There is only your perception of those.

Duality Consciousness

By the very nature of our physicality, we have what is known as duality consciousness. This is basically the dichotomy between the physical self and the indwelling spirit. This is belief in the illusion of separation. This is belief in God, Spirit, Creator, or similar as being a separate entity or not existing at all. It is a refusal to see the truth.

When you're steeped in duality consciousness, anything you're trying to manifest you're creating from the self, the ego self, and the "I" aspect of yourself, rather than with the truth of co-creating from a place of oneness.

Duality consciousness is the consciousness that blames, scorekeeps, judges, labels, and refuses to take responsibility for creating. This labeling and judging takes place from the platform of learned patterns and systems of belief. Manifesting becomes limited due to attempting to manifest and create with and from one's own will rather than the alignment of the ego self with the higher selves and the higher purpose.

In attempting to manifest from a place of duality consciousness, we are creating from a basis of illusion. It ultimately will not work or will work in a limited way because it is intrinsically limited in its base consciousness.

Karma

The concept of karma is often misunderstood and misinterpreted. If we think about the concept of karma with our linear minds, punishment is what we come up with. If we think about the concept of karma with our spirits, karma becomes more like a balance sheet, a reflection, and an opportunity for growth and transformation.

There is a huge difference. If you think your current issues are about karma they probably are not. They are about patterns. Try to let go of the mindset that says, "I'm bad and I'm being punished." This keeps the focus on "I."

Shift the perspective into, "What do I need to examine about my patterns or the patterns of those people that I allow into my life?" This shifts the focus to forward moving energy.

Entitlement

Entitlement is the belief system that someone or something owes you something for the trouble you've been through or the things you've endured. This is a barrier to manifesting because when we feel we are entitled to something we are stuck in our ego. And we cannot manifest from a place of ego. Being in entitlement turns you into a victim and renders you powerless.

If you feel that you are the victim of a bad childhood, bad relationship, bad circumstances, or similar, that is where you stay, a victim. If you feel that someone owes you something for that – particularly in the form of money – you are creating the illusion of limitation and insisting that reparation show up in a certain way. To insist so is to give your real power of creation away. And you are asking someone else to define your own self-worth.

29

You will continue to attract similar situations and energies until you learn to forgive. And keep in mind that true forgiveness is not something we do with just the linear mind. We must do it with our spirit as well.

In forgiveness you release yourself from bonds that keep you stuck in patterns of victimhood and release yourself from the need for entitlement. This frees up your own ability and divine right to create.

We come in with nothing. We leave with nothing and we are responsible for creating everything in-between. Unless you are a minor child or helpless infant, you are entitled to nothing. Free yourself.

The Illusion of Separation

The illusion of separateness is inherent by virtue of being in physical bodies to begin with. We don't see each other as spirit. We see each other through physical eyes as physical beings. So, it is easy to get lost in the idea of that physicality being "reality." We are in fact spirit having physical experiences in a physical body, rather than physical beings trying to "get" spiritual.

If you begin to see the truth of that, you can begin to remember your oneness, wholeness, and connectedness. When you start actually living that truth, it won't seem like a strange concept to you. It will become your reality. You will begin to remember who you are, thus calling your whole spirit back to you and along with it all of your power of manifesting and creating.

Here is an example of the illusion: Any woman who has been pregnant remembers quite well being completely and totally connected to her child that she is hosting and growing and nurturing inside her.

During this time mother and child are "one." It doesn't mean they are the same person or entity. (i.e., I am not God) But they are one. They are connected.

I am not the Creator, but I have the ability to create.

After giving birth there is now an illusion of separateness between them. However, any mother can also tell you that even after the cord is cut physically they are never truly separate. They are always connected.

Now here is the important part: The mother remembers full well this connection – both while carrying the child and afterward as well. She remembers it forever. It is the child who perceives itself as separate. It is the child who does not remember the connection and sometimes does not want to remember the connection because it wants to do whatever it wants to do.

So much of our journey here on Earth is perception. Despite what the mind may tell us, we were not dropped off here without ability to communicate. We are not alone. Everyone has this ability to reconnect.

Everyone has intuition and everyone has the ability to co-create and manifest exactly what they desire. Remembering your connection is a basic foundation for being able to do that effectively.

The Illusion of Limitation

There is always a way to get something accomplished, and often there is more than one way. We tend to problem solve from the perspective of our ingrained belief system or from the illusion of what we think we see or what we think we know. Based on this one might believe they are limited.

The inner dialogue plays an important part in the illusion of limitation. If you believe you are limited, then you are limited. When we let go of the conscious thoughts of the linear mind, we open a pathway to possible solutions.

And now we know that the energy of that ingrained belief system is in the root chakra. When the mind is able to supersede the illusions and constraints of the belief system of the root, anything can be accomplished.

Here is a basic example: You routinely exercise at a small gym. There are two treadmills and one medium size electric fan. When you use the treadmill you like to have the fan blowing on you. The fan is plugged into a nearby outlet in the wall. The fan is situated just so, to be able to blow on you while you're exercising.

One day you go to the gym and discover there are now four treadmills instead of two. You eye them suspiciously like unwelcome invaders. But then you see the sense of having more treadmills in there. Your mind acclimates to the idea, and you're ready to begin your workout.

The fan is in the same place as it always was, but the treadmill you like to use is now far away from the fan. You're not up for trying one of the new treadmills because you are familiar with the old one, you know how to operate it, and that's what you're comfortable with.

You have a fleeting moment of panic when you realize that the fan does not now extend

34

close to the treadmill you want to use. The cord is too short. You make a cursory examination of the other walls. You do see another outlet, but it's full. The cord for the TV is plugged into the socket and some of the new treadmills are plugged in there as well. The fan's breeze will not reach you. You tell yourself you will just accept that and do your workout anyway because you don't see any way to get the fan to blow on you now.

You begin to walk on your treadmill, simply accepting the situation because that is who you are. You are easy going, a non-complainer; and you have learned to simply accept things. Your inner dialogue and belief system is one in which you just deal with whatever comes along.

You are really perspiring now, being fifteen minutes into your routine. And you think to yourself that you may just cut the exercise session short if you don't cool down a bit.

During the fifteen minutes you have been walking you find that you've let your linear mind wander a little. You look around the room and you notice a small cupboard that you never noticed before. There isn't a lock on it. You stop your workout, get off the treadmill, and cautiously open the cupboard. You quickly peek inside. You don't want to do anything wrong.

Inside is an extension cord which is long enough to reach from an empty outlet located on another wall, to the fan, and over to your machine. You now have the tool to be able to produce your desired breeze. But you now have to actually DO something with it. You have to plug it in.

Now here is something important: By your sheer will you may be able to manifest someone else coming in the room and plugging it in for you. This is ultimately limiting as well. Eventually you will have to be willing to do things yourself in order to get the desired result in a lasting and consistent manner. Doing so brings you out of entitlement.

Fifteen Million Dollars

Let's say that you've read all the current ideas on manifesting. You decide that as part of your positive thinking and law of attraction process that you will implement these teachings by writing out a check to yourself for the money that you desire to come to you. It's a symbol of wealth and success to you. You make the check out for fifteen million dollars and you put it in a place where you can see it and think about it every day. And maybe you even say affirmations regarding these millions of dollars coming to you. You fully expect this to manifest because you believe that by your will and your visualizations and positive affirmations that it will.

Ultimately nothing happens and you wonder why you can't make any money. What is wrong here? First of all, we don't "make" money. We create a flow and open pathways so that the energy of money can flow to us.

Secondly, it may seem incongruous to your linear mind, but by putting a limit (fifteen million) however high that amount may seem to you, you have just effectively limited yourself to the fifteen million dollars that you are trying to manifest. Instead of opening a pathway to this, you have created limitation. Limitation is an illusion. We cannot effectively manifest from an illusion. We manifest from the place of truth.

There is another reason why this doesn't work. This is because you've done it with only one part of yourself. You've done it with the power of your linear mind. And saying affirmations and thinking positive thoughts about it come from that same chakra – the mind chakra. The processes you are using to manifest, even if they are multiple processes, are coming from only one chakra.

The energy of money resides in the root chakra, not in the sixth chakra.

You must bring up the energy of money from the chakra that it resides in – the chakra of creation – through all of the balanced, clear, and aligned chakras and into the sixth chakra and then let it go up and out through both the sixth and seventh chakras so that it may return to you. You must create it on another level other than linear, and then let it go so that it may return to you. You have now freed this energy up so the universe can bring you what you want.

Illusions of the Linear Mind – Perceptions

The Khaki Shorts

One key to manifesting is to free yourself from limited thinking and limited thought processes. This is where the mind fools the rest of the body into accepting as truth what it thinks it sees and knows based on what it thinks it sees. Expand your mind and thus expand your ability to manifest.

Here is another example of limited thinking: Figure out how to expand your thoughts as you think about this situation.

Let's say there is someone you see every day. This is an older gentleman and you see him on the walking trail where you take your daily walk. Being the observant person that you are, you notice that this man is wearing the same thing every day, khaki shorts and a white pullover shirt.

You wonder why. He seems clean and neat and you are walking in an affluent neighborhood.

Then you see him in the grocery store and other places around town and he is wearing the same clothing. Now you're really curious. You do not understand why this person only has one outfit when he can probably afford other clothing.

One day he asks you to help him pack for a trip he is taking. You agree to help, but you think to yourself, "What is to pack? A pair of shorts and a white shirt?"

You ponder this as you drive over to his house on the appointed day. You expect that you will be out of there in very short order.

As you enter the walk-in closet in preparation for packing, you suddenly see the truth. This person has twenty pairs of khaki shorts and twenty of the same white shirt. He isn't wearing the same clothing every day. It only appears as if he is.

If you ask him why he wears these look-alike clothes, you might learn something that helps expand your mind even further.

When we limit ourselves to one point of view or judge a book by its cover, we are limiting ourselves in other ways as well. Expand.

Person A and Person B

Person A and Person B live in what most would consider a retirement community. On the freeway, quite near the exit ramp, Person B suddenly speeds up and crosses in front of Person A, who is ambling along prudently just under the speed limit. Person B then exits the freeway with this maneuver.

This episode does not cause any physical harm to Person A. However, it stays with her long enough afterward to put some valuable time and energy into writing an indignant letter to her local newspaper. The gist of her letter is that she cannot understand why a retired person would be in such a rush to cut in front of her like that.

Irrespective of whether or not Person B was wrong in this action, Person A is only seeing things from her limited parameter. Person A is coming from her own perspective. Person A is not seeing that Person B performed this seemingly erratic and unnecessary (from Person A's point of view) maneuver for a reason, other than to startle her, make her angry, or whatever else Person A was feeling.

Person A is also making the assumption that, like her, Person B is retired. The truth is Person B is not retired. Person A is very attached to how Person B made her feel. These are Person A's issues. They do not belong to Person B.

Person B is completely oblivious to how Person A is feeling anyway. Person B has their own agenda as well. Person B is a paramedic called suddenly to the scene of an emergency. Unknown to Person A at the time is that one of her friends is involved as a potential victim in the emergency. Person B ends up saving her life.

Things are not always what they seem. It is when we are able to step out of our own ego centered viewpoints, illusions, and limitations, that the truth can begin to reveal itself to us. And when we have the truth we can manifest.

The Illusion of Time

Time is not linear. Time is multi-dimensional. However, most of us have come to perceive time as linear. It's an illusion; but as we go about our daily lives, we don't view it that way. We are taught to view it as linear because that is what works best here in the earthbound illusion. We have learned to function well with the concept of time being linear. And that is what we've come to accept as truth.

Here we will take a linear concept such as time and use it to open up a pathway to something that is not linear. This is an exercise in beginning to open up another pathway so that you can begin to manifest what you want.

Look at the time on a real clock. I'm talking about a real clock, not a digital clock with LED numbers. Close your eyes and get a firm picture of what time it is on the clock. When you can see the actual clock in your mind, open your eyes and go do something else for forty-five minutes to an hour.

When you find yourself wondering what time it is, do NOT look at a clock. Close your eyes; see the clock that you looked at before. And in your mind's eye, SEE with your "eyes" what time it is now. Then you can open your physical eyes, look at an actual clock, and get confirmation as to what you saw in your mind.

When you are able to do this with accuracy, you have taken your perception of something linear (illusion) and turned it into the truth.

Lucky

Lucky was working the morning shift at the diner and she was already exhausted from the tragic events of the night before. But being the survivor that she was, she would plod along as she always did.

Last night her new boyfriend had fallen asleep with a lit cigarette. Before she knew it her cute little house with the mountain view had burned down along with all her stuff. She got out okay, but her dogs and cats had run off howling and shrieking into the night. And her poor little bird, which she had named Lucky Too died in the horrible sooty mess. She hoped to God it wasn't a sign.

Needless to say, she broke up with the boyfriend last night. She wasn't that into him anyway. She had just wanted the sex and the little stuff he brought her. Obviously he was completely worthless. Her father used to ask, "Where do you find these people? Under a rock?"

The boyfriend really hadn't contributed much in the way of money as he should have. Why shouldn't he contribute? The sex was good between them. She definitely knew what she was doing in that department.

But he had his own problems. He had a half-baked flooring business. He hadn't been paying his subcontractors because he'd already spent the deposits he collected from the customers on gambling, alcohol and who knows what else. His life was in shambles like the pile of black rubble that used to be her home.

To make matters worse, her parents had co-signed for her loan and she was already two months behind in the payments, because, after all, there was only one of her to go around and she already was working as hard as she could. Four days a week was all she could manage with that bad back of hers. What did they expect of her anyway?

Under the circumstances someone might think the fire was suspicious and the insurance might not pay. The whole thing made her nervous and nauseous. Great! All she needed was an anxiety attack now and she might even get fired to top things off. She quickly popped a mild tranquilizer into her mouth. She was dying for a cigarette, but her break wasn't for another hour.

Her silent mantra was, "I work a lot of hours and I don't make any money." And it was true. People just didn't tip the way they should! As a whole they were rude and ungrateful creatures.

All she really wanted was to write a best-selling novel. Was that too much to ask? She was trying to do something about it too. She had just returned from a writer's conference. It was something she couldn't afford to do, but she did it anyway.

She was a small girl, but she had a very big dream that would get her out of here. But she had no computer now and it would be a while before she could save up enough money for another one. The dream would take a little more time.

Maybe she would even be the next J.K. Rowling. Things like that still happened. Yes they did. She believed they did. She had even written to J.K. for advice but received a very nasty reply from an assistant. Well, it wasn't J.K.'s fault she had such ignorant people working for her. Perhaps she didn't even know it.

When she became rich and famous, she would be in control of everything and everyone that worked for her. She would be in touch with it all.

"Hey Lucky, any chance of getting lucky today?" She gave the old man asking the question a half smile that didn't make it to her china blue eyes.

"No, Joe, not with me, but I'll bring your pancakes in a minute. Extra butter. For luck."

Curses on her alcoholic lunatic of a mother who had saddled her with this ridiculous name! She was tired of the jokes. Tired of it all. She would get out of here! She would!

She even had a little song that she sang over and over to herself in her head. It was about luck. It was about her. She was superstitious as hell. She believed in luck, good and bad; and she'd decided that her luck was definitely bad.

But luck was luck and at some point it would turn around. She wasn't named Lucky for absolutely no reason was she? She was definitely an optimist and she believed in "someday" with all her heart.

All she needed was a little break from all the bad things that kept happening to her. Just a little break to catch her breath. Was that too much to ask? She didn't know exactly why these things kept happening. If she really thought about it she had a tale of woe a few miles long. She learned to expect this bad luck as a matter of course. In her mind she always prepared for it like an unwelcome pop-in guest knocking on the door. It's why she always made her bed first thing in the morning. One never knew what would come calling.

She was a very responsible person and she believed in being forearmed. It was better than being caught with no underwear on in case you got in a car accident. This latest episode was the worst though. She just attributed it all to bad karma. Perhaps she'd been a serial killer in a previous life.

It could have all been worse, she supposed. Ever the optimist, she told herself she still had the mountain view.

Chakra Balance and Stuck Energy

We dwell in our physical bodies, which we can see, feel, and touch and are aware of; but we also have our spiritual body, aura, or etheric bodies/energy field, which we may or may not be aware of. This is where the chakras are, in the auric field of the etheric body which surrounds the physical body.

Chakras run front to back and are connected to the spine and they spin clockwise. Each chakra carries particular energy. Each chakra is a different color. And each chakra vibrates to different sounds, words, and affirmations. Just as we care for the physical body, we should also attend to the chakras. This should be as natural as brushing one's teeth.

Just as energy gets stuck on meridian points, so does energy get stuck in chakras. If energy is stuck in chakras, we find ourselves stuck in the issues that relate to those particular chakras. It is no different than stuck energy causing disease in the physical body. When energy is stuck in chakras, we can find ourselves dealing over and over again with the same issues and wondering why and how to move out of those patterns.

How do we clear and/or balance our chakras, thus clearing our energy and thus helping us get unstuck from certain issues? And what and where are the issues?

There are several ways to clear the energy of the chakras and none of them are particularly difficult. The method you will learn here is easy and pleasurable. First become aware of each chakra and become familiar with what issues reside in which chakras. This is helpful in a way that a schematic is helpful. It gives you a visual, a blueprint for something that you cannot "see."

Each chakra has a unique consciousness of its own. Once you become familiar with each you will be able to move on to learning how to clear and balance them.

First Chakra Yantra

The First Chakra

In the first chakra are issues regarding money, sex, tribe, family, self-worth, and addiction and distortions regarding such. Also in this chakra is the energy of control issues, basic survival, self-acceptance, and group acceptance. The energy of abuse and self-abuse, prosperity, perception, grounding, primal fear and safety, superstitions, mental stability, physical health and stability and victim energy also resides here. Additionally, in this chakra lives groundedness and connection to the earth, abandonment issues as they relate to both parents, prosperity, trust, ability to relax and the divine right to create.

Anything that relates to the "root of the matter" resides here. Someone with root chakra blockages and issues may appear to have anxiety, control issues revolving around safety, a general sense of flakiness, spaciness, or inability to focus or concentrate. Also, they may appear to have relationship issues in the form of moving from one partner to another and just wanting sex for the sake of the physical release. They may have allergies or other related health issues, distortions of reality and distortions of perception regarding relationships, childhood issues, sexual performance issues and entitlement.

As you can see, there is a lot going on in there. The color of the root chakra is red and it is located at the base of the spine facing toward the earth.

Second Chakra Yantra

The Second Chakra

In the second chakra are issues around birthing, getting an idea out to the world and to the marketplace, creativity in general, and creative expression of all kinds. Also, in this chakra are female issues as they relate to motherhood, the concept of motherhood, and mother-child relationships.

To me the father-child relationship resides in the first chakra; but it sometimes spills over into the second chakra, depending upon whether or not you incarnated into this particular lifetime as male or female. Remember, all of the chakras are connected, just as your leg or arm is connected to your physical body. They are not just energy centers unto themselves.

Also in the second chakra are issues of sexuality, emotions revolving around sexuality, financial creativity, and integrity especially as it relates to financial transactions, honor and bravery.

The "not good enough" or "something's wrong with me" energy resides here. This is where we see people who have been sexually abused and then go to counseling, emerge from that process and think they've done their forgiveness work, or their acceptance work. And perhaps they have, however they've just done it on one level – the physical level. And then they find they cannot create money flow in their lives and do not know why. This forgiveness and acceptance work must also be done in the spiritual realm in order for it to integrate and filter through all of the energy centers. People with blockages in this chakra often feel the world or group/ organization, company or business owes them something.

In a woman with second chakra issues, we see things like fibroids and ovarian cysts manifesting in the physical body. Both sexes have abandonment issues. (Abandonment issues reside in the first chakra as well as in the second chakra.) In both men and women with second chakra blocks, we see disappointment and anger at non-perfection or one's idea, perception, or illusion of perfection. This relates to the self and/or to one's life partner or significant other, to one's co-workers, family, etc. There is a distorted and unrealistic view of the concept of perfection.

The color of the second chakra is orange and it is located in the pelvic area. Remember, chakras are cone shaped, connected to the spine at the more pointed end, and are in both the front and the back of the physical body.

Third Chakra Yantra

The Third Chakra

In the third chakra we have issues of digestion as they relate to one's ability to "digest" or accept their lifetime and/or their choices. Sometimes these issues overlap and spill into the first and second chakras as well. For example, someone that is having difficulty accepting themselves or their journey here will often have stomach/ digestive issues which eventually can turn into colon issues, i.e., the inability to get rid of what no longer serves them.

The third chakra area (solar plexus) is where the soul resides. It is the seat of the will. Self-esteem, vitality, zest for life, and life purpose live here. It is the chakra where the individual feels the need to express oneself. If there are blocks in this chakra, the expression of self may present as somewhat wacky, unbalanced, and unstable, rather than as slightly eccentric and charmingly individual.

We may also see someone who is arrogant and manipulative, stubborn, and attached to being right. This is the chakra where denial lives and this is where blame and scorekeeping originates.

The sense of humor may be warped, offbeat, and not easily understood by others. The sense of self is distorted and there is a feeling of not being able to connect with others on any level. Narcissism may be predominant, but the individual believes they are the nicest person that ever lived. They are blinded by their own reflection.

In persons with third chakra issues, we often see role reversal and a strong belief that they are being punished. Young people that have been caretakers to their parents often have these kinds of third chakra issues.

Those with third chakra blocks sometimes have excessive caution, inertia and inability to make a decision, and the feeling that they have bad luck or karma and are victims of circumstances.

They may also exhibit refusal to take responsibility and acknowledge their free will choices and decisions, preferring to make someone else into the responsible party. There is also a tendency to have bursts of anger and a general feeling of being mad at the world.

The color of the third chakra is yellow and it is located in the solar plexus, the center of the physical body.

Fourth Chakra Yantra

The Fourth Chakra

In the fourth chakra are issues of the heart. Here we find issues of intimacy (which also spill over into the root/first chakra), issues of trust, issues of honesty, compassion, issues of being able to express and receive love on different levels than through the first chakra.

Sometimes we see this distorted energy spilling over into the fifth chakra as issues with communication of feelings and the ability to express those verbally. A person with heart chakra blocks will have confusion as to how to express love in general, will be wary of those that do so freely, will dislike the act of hugging unless they initiate it

61

themselves, and can seem cold, distant, and emotionally withholding.

We also see jealousy, envy, possessiveness, and co-dependent relationships in people with fourth chakra blocks. They have trouble making boundaries and understanding and honoring the boundaries and emotions of others. There is also a tendency to take everything personally and there is an "I" centered point of view.

People with blockages in this chakra have trouble with the concept of giving and receiving. They may be able to grasp it with their mind, know on some level that they should give and receive. But they may have a difficult time putting it into practice. They have trouble establishing a balanced flow of this energy.

The belief in limitation lives in this chakra. People with blocked heart chakra energy can become easily depressed, unforgiving, intolerant of others, and stuck in their perceptions of the world, which they may view as harsh.

The color of the heart chakra is emerald green and it is located in the center of the chest.

Fifth Chakra Yantra

The Fifth Chakra

In the fifth chakra lives the energy of communication. When the energy of this chakra is blocked, the communication challenges may show up in a lot of different ways depending upon what other chakras have blocked or stagnant energies.

Blocked energy here may show up as the inability to listen and process what others are saying. People with energy blockages here may talk too much, too fast, or not at all. They may have a weak, timid, or hesitating voice.

They may be critical and insist on things being done their way or not at all. They may be prone to sore throats and laryngitis.

They may have a tendency to gossip, or they may be verbally abusive. A person with fifth chakra issues may be prone to headaches, ear aches, and neck pain as well.

Thyroid issues or extreme fatigue may surface in people with blocked fifth chakra energy. Putting feelings into words may be challenging and a fear of public speaking may be evident. A sense of rhythm and timing may be affected by stagnant energy in this chakra. An ongoing challenge and goal is to speak one's truth.

The color of the fifth chakra is blue. It is located in the center of the throat.

Sixth Chakra Yantra

The Sixth Chakra

The sixth chakra is often called the third eye. Here we have the energy of intuitiveness, cognitive knowingness, telepathic ability, spatial and full clairvoyance, and forward moving, transformative energy of the spirit/spiritual path.

Most importantly, here we have the ability to transform the lower into the higher. It is in this chakra that the energy that rises up from the root chakra, along with the energy of the other chakras, has the opportunity to transform into true and clear vision and become manifest in the physical world.

If someone has blocks in this chakra, for example, we may see them being non-accepting of their intuitive abilities or of

65

their ability to connect to Source. There may even be a non-belief in Source.

When this chakra is ignored or denied, we see this presenting as an inability to remember dreams, inability to focus or concentrate fully, and poor memory.

Children that evidence psychic ability early in life are often told that they are imagining things and thus they learn to block the energy of this powerful chakra and focus instead on root chakra activities. They may experiment with drugs or alcohol.

It is here in the sixth chakra that clear vision and perceptions have opportunity to turn into earthly reality. If the perceptions of the lower chakras are distorted, the energy of this chakra cannot clearly make manifest the truth and the individual remains stuck in illusion and distortion wondering why they cannot manifest.

Meditation strengthens this chakra as well as dream work, journaling, drawing, painting, and other creative expressions such as the use of yantras and mantras.

The sixth chakra is located in the middle of the forehead and its color is indigo.

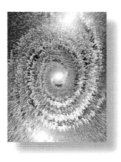

Seventh Chakra Yantra

The Seventh Chakra

The seventh chakra is the crown chakra. Here is the energy of universal oneness, creation, wholeness, trust, wisdom, spiritual awareness, knowledge and truth. This chakra is easy to find. Think about when babies come into the world. They have that baby soft spot on the top of their heads. That is where the crown chakra is. Babies come in with this chakra open and fully trusting.

The soft spot closes as the spirit fully in-carnates and seats into this earthly realm and into its physical body and the person begins to be connected more through the root chakra. In a way, the closing over of the crown chakra is initially for protection. But ultimately people that remain spiritually unaware become very untrusting, suspicious, and closed minded.

Here in the consciousness of this chakra is our true life purpose and our ability to connect with that and with all that is with an open mind.

The color of the seventh chakra is violet and/or white and/or gold.

+ + + + + + + +

In general, those are the issues. If you find yourself stuck in a particular issue or recurring theme, try to identify which chakra or chakras this might relate to. This can be a place on which to focus for the clearing and balancing of the chakras.

Again, chakras are interconnected; and when we have a blockage in one, there can also be blockages/stagnant energy in others. Keep in mind, as well, that our etheric bodies/energy field is not just on one level. There are many layers. The energy field is as multi-dimensional as you are.

Yantras and Mantras

The simplified explanation of a yantra is a drawing or symbol that serves as a meditative focal point for connecting the mind and body with the spirit. A yantra serves to draw the external mind into internal connection. The yantra helps shift the consciousness from the external world to the internal world.

A yantra represents the body. Yantras are tools to transform the energy of the lower chakras (the body) into the higher energy necessary for transformation. It is helpful to draw one's own yantras as it helps teach the mind to focus and concentrate.

The simplified explanation of a mantra is a series of syllables or words that when intoned together serve to open the chakras, expand the mind, and facilitate energy flow. A mantra represents the intentions of the mind and will of the spirit.

All sound, like words and music, has vibration; and vibration has the ability to transform. Sound is a carrier of energy. When you transform your thoughts into physical words or syllables and then speak them, those vibrations become vehicles of the thoughts and intentions to being made manifest.

When yantras and mantras are used together, they serve to connect the left brain and right brain – both hemispheres of the brain – open up the energy of the chakras, and serve as a tool to the ultimate goal of the connection of mind, body, and spirit. And that's what we're doing here, connecting the dots so you can manifest whatever you desire.

The yantras pictured in this book are made from the seven doors in *Voice of the Angels – A Healing Journey Spiritual Cards* and represent the seven chakras that we are working with now. The mantras are verses from the cards. The original artwork was made with crystals and other natural elements. They were not computer generated and thus carry with them intrinsically different core energy than similar decks. The reason we are using them here is as initial focal points for clearing and balancing the chakras. Eventually, you may want to draw your own.

Every chakra has a corresponding sound, syllable, or mantra that activates the energy of that chakra. We can equate that here with affirmations, which are basically whole positive thoughts as opposed to syllables, said aloud or written on a piece of paper with intention of transformation.

Whether you're saying them aloud or writing them down, what you're doing is taking an initial thought and transforming it from an abstract into a more solid form. Whenever you're engaging your thoughts with your actions, you have the power of transformation and manifestation.

When Annie Sullivan was attempting to teach the deaf, mute, and blind Helen Keller, she made motions and impressions with her fingers into Helen's hand. She was trying to teach Helen that every motion had a meaning and the meaning corresponded to something tangible. It was not until she poured the actual water onto Helen's hand while finger signing simultaneously did Helen finally make the connection that the finger signing actually was the representation for the word "water." This connection transformed Helen's life and countless other lives as well.

71

When we do not understand what someone is trying to teach us or the real meaning behind the lesson, we remain in the dark.

Thus is the power of yantras and mantras. It is a multidimensional rather than linear way of implementing and learning the ability to manifest.

Here are mantra syllables, affirmations, and mantras that will activate the energy of each chakra:

First Chakra (Base Chakra): LAM

I am committed to staying on earth and doing what I came here to do. I realize everything is a lesson in Love. I am free to create.

"The first door is for grounding and connecting to the earth. The cords are just connection to help you then give birth."

Second Chakra (Sacral Chakra): VAM

I am deserving of feeling pleasure in a healthy way. I am not alone. I am able to create all that I need.

"Door two is almost open now and its orange is truly bright. This color will assist you dear in shining out your radiant light."

Third Chakra (Solar Plexus Chakra): RAM

I am grounded. I am relaxed. I am powerful. I replace feelings of inadequacy with hope, love, light, inspiration, faith, and joy.

"The third door here is beautiful and golden yellow like the sun. It reminds you gently now that we really are all one."

Fourth Chakra (Heart Chakra): YAM

I am worthy. I am safe. I am loved. I am valuable. I vibrate to the frequency of Love.

"Emerald green so soothing now is what's at the center of this door. So focus now on healing all emotions deep within your core."

Fifth Chakra (Throat Chakra): HAM

I am the expression of truth. I am free to speak my truth.

"Communication is what speaks to you through this door of blue. Listen carefully now and hear just what is being conveyed to you."

Sixth Chakra (Third Eye): Ham-Ksham

I am aware and accept that everything in the universe is knit together and works for the highest good. It is my divine right to manifest my vision. I am wisdom.

"Indigo is for opening and seeing what's not there. This door is fully open how if you only dare."

Seventh Chakra (Crown Chakra): AUM – OM

I am open minded. I am willing. I am light. I am able to detach and release from what I think I want. I am free.

"This door is made of violet and total pure white light. It enables you to see the truth even when it's night."

Elayne

Elayne untwisted her slender body from its graceful contortion and stood up to dismiss the last yoga class of the evening with her usual and cheerful "Namaste." She'd had enough downward facing dogs today to last two lifetimes. She was weary to her very bones and just wanted to get home to the peaceful solitude of her little trailer.

She didn't know exactly why she was so tired and she wondered idly if she had cancer or something. No, she told herself, that was impossible. She was far too healthy from the strict vegetarian diet and all the vitamins and supplements she consumed on a daily basis. Her caramel brown colored complexion positively glowed, didn't it? Everyone said so. Granted they weren't top of the line supplements because she couldn't afford those, but they worked just as well she suspected. No cancer for this health nut. She was a survivor. She'd survived everything and would continue to do so.

She gathered her worn leather handbag and keys from her locker, shut off all the lights, locked the door behind her, and made her way through the dark parking lot to her rusty old car.

Ever vigilant with one hand on her pepper spray, she quickly unlocked the car, got in, and turned the key in the ignition. Nothing. *Damn it all to hell.* She wasn't going to spend money on a tow truck. She didn't need another expense at this point. This would have to wait for now. She'd spend the night at the yoga studio. She'd done it before. It was fine she told herself. She'd be safe. "I am safe everywhere in the universe." She repeated the affirmation aloud even if there wasn't one exhausted bone in her thin as a rail body that believed it. Well, it couldn't hurt.

She made her way back across the cracked black pavement and fumbled anxiously with the keys in the lock of the studio door. It was slightly sticky and she was impatient as she glanced apprehensively over her shoulder. She just wanted to get back in. Being alone and exposed like this in the shadowy night, however briefly, brought back those unwanted and haunting memories of ice cold steel against her bare skin. *And more.* She shuddered as the door finally opened and she slammed it hard and locked it behind her with a loud thud and a huge sigh of relief. Someone really ought to fix that thing.

Small pangs of hunger assaulted her toned and taut stomach as she made her way into the tiny but adequately stocked kitchen to make a small tabouli salad. She was used to them, though. She never ate much and this would be the first real meal of the day. She'd had a nutrition bar sometime this morning. For her, eating was usually automated and utilitarian.

She was grateful now that the wheat for the salad was already soft and all she had to do was mix in some other ingredients. As she chopped some fresh parsley and cucumber with the sharp steel of a knife, those disturbingly haunting memories from the past bubbled up to the surface again like primordial ooze. She tried unsuccessfully to stuff them back down, but they didn't want to go. She felt like she was going to vomit. Shouldn't people be able to be safe within the confines of their own minds?

Even though it was over four years ago, being brutally attacked, raped, thrown on the side of the road, and left for dead by three disgusting, putrid men seemed as fresh and raw as the tomato she was now chopping.

Since then she'd lost everything including her marriage and she hadn't had a relationship since. *She just couldn't.* What galled her tender black woman's soul the most was that those boys had gotten off with a silly slap on the wrist. And now they were out there again somewhere. . . lurking in the night.

She'd taken self-defense classes soon after and those became a catalyst to collecting certifications in every healing modality that she could. She was certified in so many she had lost count. She could Zero Balance and Reikify and Healing Touch anyone. This had naturally segued into learning and then teaching yoga. Yoga was supposed to be healing and balancing and it was. In the aftermath of all the destruction, she had soaked up the learning like a dry and thirsty sponge. It had kept her sane and helped her re-ground and had given her a sense of peace. And now she had a whole lot of pieces of paper that told her who she was and a growing reputation for being the best yoga instructor around.

Too bad those pieces of paper and all that training weren't converting into dollars though. Why oh why couldn't she make any money? In fact, if things didn't turn around soon, she'd have to close the studio. She didn't understand what the problem was. She'd used the services of that highly recommended Feng Shui expert recently. He was brilliant. He was an expert in transforming the energy of any room. Such a gift! His magic touch was quickly becoming legendary and everyone knew he didn't charge as much as he could.

Even so, it was a stretch for her financially; but she was able to split it between the last few credit cards that were hovering just under her spending limit. He was so sweet and even had done some "cures" for free. Bless his gay little soul. Well, why not? Elayne was a giver. She gave, gave, gave all the time to everyone, so certainly this was just part of what was owed to her by the universe anyway. His work was guaranteed.

However if it didn't start working soon, she'd be seeking a refund.

But she had a plan B. She always had a plan B. She'd started a small magazine, *Yoga Time*, from her newsletter and student base. It wasn't New York slick and glossy the way she wanted it just yet because money was so tight. But someday it would be and when she struck it rich from whatever the good Lord had in store for her down the road, she would make it so.

If only she hadn't helped put that ungrateful ex-husband of hers through medical school. She would never understand why she had to end up with half of those debts as her own. Was there no fairness in the world? And after all that, he chose a chiropractic specialty. She rolled her eyes in disgust. Whatever. If she ever threw her back out with all her upside-down and twisty contortions, he owed her a free adjustment or two. *Uh huh. For sure.*

Elayne took a few bites of her salad, but she wasn't hungry anymore. Life in general was just distasteful. She opened the drawer where she kept the neatly folded used aluminum foil. No sense in wasting anything. She had to be frugal.

She covered what was left of the salad and bent down to open the door to the mini refrigerator. Not much of anything in there and the cold air was like a smack in the face. Yes, the Lord certainly owed her something too, didn't He? *Plan, reveal thyself.* She could hardly wait.

Chakra Balancing – Part I

Now that you know what energy resides in each chakra and what consciousness dwells in each, you can begin to balance, clear, and align your chakra system.

Some of you may already know how to balance and clear your chakras. However, if they were truly clear, balanced, and aligned, you probably wouldn't be reading this book.

The goal is to get everything working together in a state of synchronicity and we can't accomplish that if the chakras aren't aligned with the will. The ultimate goal is to attain a state of balance such that you have only to say or think something and it then manifests immediately.

The very first thing to do to prepare for chakra balancing is to get comfortable. You can clear and balance your chakras either sitting up with the spine straight or lying down. Get in the position that feels most natural for you. However you want to have your spine as straight as possible.

You will go into a relaxed state by using breathing techniques. You will ground and center yourself. You will clear and spin each chakra as you connect them with your breath, your intention, and your visualization. Then you will bring that energy up, out, and around and back through your body.

The yantra helps with centering and focus and the mantra and breath help with clearing the energy. Visualize the yantra for each chakra and say the mantra syllable either aloud or in your mind for each chakra while you are clearing.

Breathing and Relaxation Techniques

Each person must ultimately find the combination or technique that works most effectively for them. You won't know what that is until you try. The goal is to achieve a relaxed state of being where you have quieted the chatter of the conscious mind, you are mindfully aware of your breath, and you can feel more of a connection with your spirit rather than your physical body.

My personal preference for meditation is a combination of prana breathing followed by a sequence of breathing to a count of four (inhale), seven (hold), eight (exhale), and then sliding smoothly into a pattern of slow and deep breathing, inhaling deeply through the nose with a definitive exhale through the mouth. Explore and find what works best for you.

Prana Breathing

Prana breathing is also known as yoga or nostril breathing. It is an easy technique and extremely relaxing within two to three minutes. It is difficult to focus on this type of breathing and your conscious thoughts at the same time. That's why it is an effective technique and it doesn't take long to achieve the desired degree of relaxation.

To begin, place your right index finger on your right nostril, holding it closed. Keeping it closed, inhale deeply through your left nostril. Immediately place your left index finger on your left nostril, holding it closed while releasing your right nostril. Exhale through the right nostril.

Inhale back through your right nostril while holding the left nostril closed. Close the right nostril and exhale out the left. Inhale back through the left. Close it and exhale out the right. Repeat this process for two to three minutes. You will feel deeply relaxed and refreshed and your mind will be clear.

Grounding

People that are overly stressed literally feel like they are coming "unglued." This means that you are ungrounded. Grounding is simply a connection to the earth. To ground, imagine tree roots growing out of the bottoms of both your feet. Plug them deep into the ground, just like a strong tree. Connect deeply with the earth. Then pull up earth energy from the roots and into your body. You will feel energized.

If you have an aversion to connecting into the earth, you may connect into a body of water, such as the ocean or your favorite lake. And then pull up the life force energy from that body of water into your body. Whichever way you do it, you want to achieve a feeling of deep connection.

Centering

Centering is a refocusing. When you are stressed you are most likely focused on your stress or anxiety. Getting centered will help you feel less stressed and shift your focus away from an "I" centered attitude.

We want to get centered because it is from the center of the body that we align our spirit and our will. And when we are aligned energy can flow properly, thus setting the stage for manifesting.

To get centered, place your focus on the very center of your body. This is in the solar plexus area. Visualize a ball of light there. See it glowing and radiating. Imagine yourself to be in the center of yourself, or the very center of your physical body, sitting at the center of this ball of light. Really feel yourself there. Keep your focus on the ball of light for a few minutes and feel the anxiety slowly dissipating and melting away.

Now visualize a pedestal; there in the center of the ball of light. Seat yourself in the center of the pedestal; reground yourself if necessary. Keep your focus on the ball of light. You should be still sitting in the middle of the light and now in the middle of the pedestal. From your comfortable seated position take a look around you 360 degrees. Don't change your position, but look around in all directions from your mind's eye.

Now here is the tricky part. We want to be able to maintain a centeredness because being able to do so keeps us in alignment and keeps the energy that flows up from the first and second chakras in alignment with our purpose.

So while you are there in the very center of yourself, see, feel, or imagine someone or something, such as the wind, attempting to knock you off your pedestal. Picture yourself staying on point, staying steady, staying calmly seated, grounded, and centered at the very center of the ball of light while the wind or other disturbance rages around you. The goal of this exercise is to stay in your center and stay in the center of the light no matter what happens.

The energy of manifesting comes up from the lower chakras and through your center; so it's important to be in alignment. If you aren't, it is difficult for that energy to get through to the upper chakras where it needs to go in order to transform.

Create a Sanctuary

Now that you know how to get grounded and centered, you can use creative visualization to create a sanctuary. We do this first because we want to release any fears we have around being in a meditative state of being and we want a safe place in which to release those fears if they exist somewhere in our energy field. Fear blocks the ability to manifest.

Some of you may already have a sanctuary; but for purposes of this exercise, create a new one. You may even think you don't need one because you aren't afraid of anything. However, the main purpose of creating this is not about fear or safety, really.

You'll want to create a sanctuary anyway because a lot of interesting things can

92

happen there, things you wouldn't discover if you didn't create it.

Creating your sanctuary has a multitude of purposes and you won't find out what those are if you don't do it. Basically it is an exercise in expansion.

The first thing to do is to get in any position you find comfortable. Then ground yourself and center yourself in your physical body.

Visualize and run tree roots out of the bottoms of both your feet and plug them deep into the ground (or body of water). Feel yourself in the very center of your body.

Close your eyes and relax your physical body. Those that have trouble relaxing their physical bodies can try the "tense and release" technique. Simply tense all your muscles at once for about one minute and then let go all at once. Do this more than once if you're really having trouble relaxing. Doing this teaches your body on a different level the difference between tense and relaxed.

Relax and let all thoughts drift away. Begin to take long, slow, deep breaths. Focus on your breath. See and feel it entering and leaving your body. Just breathe. Relax.

Now imagine yourself in a beautiful environment. Use whatever your concept of beauty and peace is. It could be a natural environment or any other environment you find soothing and relaxing. Open your mind completely to this and visualize every detail of this beautiful place.

When you have a really clear picture of this place in your mind, thoroughly explore your environment. See, feel, know, hear everything that is going on there. Take in every detail.

Now do anything else you need to do to make this place your own. Make it comfortable and completely safe. Establish this as your own personal, private place.

You can change anything you want at any time you want simply by making it so. There are no barriers or boundaries or limitations to what you can do there. Look around and simply enjoy.

If you have any fears that come up, just leave them there, put them in a box, closet, or otherwise dispose of them.

Remember, this is your own private sanctuary from now on and you can return to it any time you desire by simply closing your eyes and being there. It will always be healing and relaxing to be there. Nothing can intrude upon you there. You are always absolutely safe, secure, and happy there.

When you come back to your physical reality, write down in a journal, draw, or otherwise describe your sanctuary and your experience there. This is so you have a clear and concrete vision of it on the physical plane.

This is another method to bring the mind, body, and spirit together in a tangible, earthly form; and it helps build and support the framework for manifesting your desires.

Nicholas

Rain was coming down by the truckload by the time Nicholas finished his late morning breakfast at the silly little off the beaten path diner he had discovered one day. No one ever followed him there. Apparently it wasn't interesting enough. But for him it was. The food was good and there was a very attractive little waitress working there. He just liked to watch her. She didn't seem to care who he was and that bothered him, but not enough to stop going there on occasion. He was drawn to her. She was sleek, just what he liked. How could she not recognize him? Maybe she just couldn't afford to go to the movies. Poor thing.

Normally he loved driving in rain, but today he had lingered a bit too long over breakfast. Now that he was done, he was in a hurry to get back home. Those narrow winding roads on the way to his house could get pretty slick. *Oh hell!* He hated being late. It made him look bad. And he never wanted to look bad. Not ever. He had an appointment with that fruity Feng Shui expert and he had to get going soon. He willed the rain to stop; and as if it really heard him, it did. He smiled to himself at his amazing power and then frowned almost simultaneously as he left money on the table for the meal and for the very pretty waitress.

His last four pictures hadn't been big at the box office. He wasn't afraid of losing his money – that could never happen to him – but he absolutely was afraid of not having the general public adore him in every way. It just wasn't acceptable. In fact, it was inconceivable to him.

Someone had suggested that there might be something wrong with the "fame" area of his home. If there was he needed it fixed *right now* and apparently this queer Bobby Dubois was the one to fix it.

The world really had gone mad. Why were there so many gay people these days? They were everywhere. Quite frankly they made him very uncomfortable. He couldn't wrap his mind around the whole gay thing. It was just wrong.

Two women now. . .that was a different story. A whole different story. He indulged in a fleeting little fantasy that included that very pretty blond waitress. She really was attractive enough to be an actress. That completely stunning blond hair was almost down to her waist. And that peachy gold skin of hers begged to be touched. Too bad she was only a waitress. He would show her a few things. It irritated him that she acted quite oblivious to his obvious charm. How could she not know who he was? And who the hell could resist him anyway? Maybe she was gay too. It seemed to be going around these days.

He got in the Jaguar and made his way toward home. This baby was as smooth as velvet. *He loved this car!* It almost purred just like a very satisfied woman and he'd had plenty of those.

For some reason he couldn't get that blond woman out of his head. He wondered what that was about. He hadn't had a real relationship since Carolyn. He didn't even know if he was capable of it. Why did women always insist on "relationships" anyway? He didn't know and it was irrelevant. He wasn't planning on having one with this waitress or anyone else. He always got what he wanted whenever he wanted it. If he wanted her he'd have her. On his terms of course.

As Nicholas came around the last winding curve before the turnoff to his beach estate, the unthinkable happened. He felt the Jag suddenly lose traction and slide out from under him. To his complete and utter horror it started skidding toward the steep cliff on the other side of the road. *Unbelievable! This could not be happening!* He was Nicholas Fortuna and he was in control at all times.

And he had always fancied himself immortal, like a cat with way more than nine lives. Like five hundred maybe. After all, he liked to think big and his luck was always astoundingly good. Certainly it hadn't run out. Weren't all gods immortal? He had an appointment with a gay man today, not the angel of death. In that strange and eerie moment between when time is suspended and reality happens he heard the crash more than felt it.

Chakra Balancing - Part II

Now that we know what energy resides in which chakras and we've learned to ground and center, we can begin to balance and clear the chakra systems. This is best done from a relaxed and meditative state. When you are fully comfortable and relaxed, you will be able to focus on your etheric body rather than your physical body. Here are the basics:

1. Relax the physical body. Release conscious thoughts.

2. Reach a meditative state through breathing techniques.

3. Ground and center yourself. Women should run a grounding cord down from the root chakra as well as the bottoms of both feet.

4. Focus on your etheric body. Just as you are able to see your physical body with your physical eyes, from a relaxed state of being you will be able to see your chakras if you open and use your third eye. The third eye is located in the center of the forehead. Open it just like you open your physical eyes and take a

101

look around. If you cannot "see" your chakras, just visualize or imagine them and the corresponding color. If you cannot see or open your third eye, just visualize it.

If you created a sanctuary (page 92), you may have met some guides and angels that will help you with this and bring you information. Do not judge any information you receive through the filter of your mind. Just listen.

5. Use your breath, your intention, and your visualization ability to clear the energy.

6. Spin each chakra clockwise, starting with the root chakra. Moving up in order, clear any dark or clogged energy with your breath and with your intention. Remember, chakras are both in the front of your body and at the back. They are cone shaped with the pointed end meeting at the spine.

7. As you move up through the chakras, open an energy pathway. Visualize or see the clear energy moving gently up the spine as you go along.

8. Connect the energy of each cleared chakra to the next one.

9. When you get to the top, the crown chakra, open it up and connect up as high as you are comfortable doing. The goal is to connect up to Source. If you do not believe in Source, connect to higher realms, upper chakras, your higher self, universal life force, a spiral, or Light.

10. Now you should be both grounded and connected and plugged in from both the top of your head and bottoms of your feet.

11. Circulate the clear energy that you've brought up through all of the chakras out through the top of the head, like a fountain. And then bring it back down and around the outside of your body. Then bring it back up through the all of the chakras, out the top of the head again, down the outside of your body and back up again through the chakras. Do this several times until you feel clear.

12. Close up the balancing and clearing work that you just did by surrounding yourself with a white/golden light.

Carlos

Carlos closed the door softly and tiptoed into the house. *God, he loved this house.* He loved everything about it and not one thing would he change. He drank in its sweet and spicy aroma. It just smelled like home, felt like home.

Ordinarily he loved coming home, but tonight he absolutely dreaded it. He ran one hand through his crisp dark hair and slowly climbed the stairs to the bedroom. He tried to figure out how he was going to deliver his distressing news to his beautiful wife, but he'd been trying to figure that out all day and still had no answer.

Maybe she already knew. His Carla just knew things. She was always with those tarot cards of hers. Or maybe those cards were the problem here. Maybe they were just evil. He shrugged his shoulders. What did he know of such things? *Nada.* And he didn't want to know either. He was a lawyer and lawyers stuck to facts. Right now he was drunk. It was a fact.

And why shouldn't he be? He was entitled. He had just flunked the bar exam for the third time. These American laws! They were estúpido. *Ridículo!*

After months of waiting he had finally gotten the results at work today. The firm was waiting anxiously for him to pass. He'd been hired contingent upon passing and had been assigned research duties. He'd been collecting a nice salary and benefits in the meantime. They had given him enough chances. Everyone had believed in him and he foolishly had believed in himself. And now he'd failed miserably. Maybe they were being punished, he and Carla, for what they had done.

He had bought this house on a dream. And now he'd been let go and maybe the dream would become a nightmare. He didn't know what he and Carla were going to do now. *Dios!* He didn't have a plan and he was scared. He didn't want to lose everything. He didn't want to lose his beautiful and exotic Carla. She thought he walked on water. He would tell her in the morning.

Patterns, Habits, Change and the Mind, Body, Spirit Team

In order to effect any change we first have to be WILLING to DO something differently. The mind must be in alignment with the will. We can then use change as a catalyst to freeing up the energy of money.

When we incarnate here we usually incarnate into a group, a family. We are then taught belief systems so that we may function together as a group or family. Those belief systems are systems that have been learned by your caretakers from their caretakers and then passed on to you as truth. Groups of people incarnate together to teach each other lessons about Love.

When you start living within these belief system structures, you then form patterns based on these belief systems. Then these patterns become ingrained and start resonating as truth to you.

When you're very young, someone first chooses your clothing for you within their framework and idea of how you ought to show up in the world. They use their own

107

idea of what looks good or feels right to them. Since you don't know anything different, you take on this "clothing" as your own. It is only after you put the clothes on and wear them for a while that they begin resonating to your energy field and become infused with your own energy.

Patterns are the result of the belief systems that you were taught and believe to be true. Habits are what is chosen as a result of resonating to these patterns.

You originally learned your core belief systems regarding success and failure and how those relate to money from your tribe. Like all other patterns, they got stuck in your root chakra and began resonating as truth through your chakra system. They became a pattern and a blueprint for your prosperity and abundance. And you have followed those patterns for a lifetime. The following of those patterns has become habit.

Both patterns and habits can be changed and shifted by the act of integrating the mind, body, and spirit, getting to the base or root of the matter, clearing, and balancing

108

the chakras and energy field, and aligning the will. And then one must accept as truth whole new belief systems and integrate them as new patterns.

Why is it so difficult or challenging to make a change, even a positive one? Part of it is because patterns and habits have become deeply ingrained in our belief systems. We may feel that making a change will fundamentally change who we are. And making a change is usually perceived as "work." Plus changing anything moves us out of our comfort zone. But it doesn't have to be so. Everything is a matter of perspective. And if you understand the illusion you can make changes instantaneously.

The first step to being comfortable with change is to start seeing your life as multi-dimensional rather than linear. What does that mean exactly? It means that your existence here isn't flat. You are not just one aspect of yourself. You are not just your body or your mind or your money.

In understanding change and becoming comfortable with the thought of imple-menting it, it is helpful to understand what is going on at a base level. You have a few different things going on here. You have your mind doing one thing – thinking thoughts. You have your body doing another thing – following the patterns that the mind has set in motion. And then you have your spirit – trying to do whatever it came here to do despite your mind's thoughts or perceptions to the contrary. When these are in conflict, we have conflict in our lives. The key to balance is to integrate all three of these so that they work together.

As an example, let's say you smoke. For those that smoke, take note that ironically the act of smoking forces you to breathe deeply, while ultimately it is the very thing that takes away your ability to breathe.

Anyway, so you smoke. The mind may reach a point where it decides it doesn't want to smoke anymore. Now, the body has been engaging in this pattern of self-abuse for however long. It's become a habit.

The physical body is addicted. Physical addiction resides in the root chakra as a very real black line of addiction. But the mind isn't addicted even though it may believe

110

that it is. And the spirit just feels suffocated by all of the smoke. You may seem stuck on the path of life. You may feel as if you're living in a fog. Forward movement may be somewhat restricted by whatever you can see and perceive through the haze.

One day the mind decides that it wants to make a change and quit smoking. Quitting becomes easier when the mind and physical body are in alignment with the goal to quit. This is probably why hypnosis works for many.

When the mind and physical body become aligned, the spirit can then shine through in purpose; and one can move forward on the path toward their life's purpose. These are the basics of mind, body, spirit integration.

Once you understand that the goal is to have the mind, body, and spirit functioning together as a team, you'll be able to make any positive change that you desire to make.

The Integration of Mind, Body, and Spirit

Most people can learn to think positively with their minds, apply the laws of attraction, open their minds enough to clear pathways to some degree, and subsequently manifest in some way. Where the trouble starts regarding being able to fully manifest is with the ability to integrate these concepts from linear thinking into conceptualized earth plane reality.

To effect positive and lasting change, the mind, body and spirit must work together as an integrated unit. The patterns must be changed, healed, and shifted at a core level. Then the new patterns can be integrated as truth.

When you're trying to implement change, implement learning and open pathways to abundance (or anything), you must understand the process. And then you must be willing to ultimately integrate the learning. That means you must DO something.

What happens first in the process is that you have a thought about what you want to create. That thought is taking place in an upper chakra. And the energy of what you're trying to create – in this case money – resides in the base chakra.

If the flow of the sixth chakra (the mind) is blocked by the static energy being generated from a basic belief system with blockage that exists in the root chakra, nothing can get translated to "paper." And money in our system is made from paper.

It is similar to a clogged pipe. It is necessary to get to the base of the matter and eliminate the obstruction that exists in the base of the pipe in order to re-establish flow.

Next, for our purposes here of learning how to manifest money, realize that you are trying to translate thought – something that is multi-dimensional or in some cases single minded – into something that's two dimensional, i.e., money/pieces of paper.

So how do we take the energy from one or two chakras and connect them in such as way to get an integrated result that manifests in physical form?

You have already learned what energy resides in which chakras and how to clear and balance them. So after you put that into practice, the next step to integration is to go back to a time before other people's belief systems became your own.

Then you clear out those belief systems so that they don't belong to you anymore. You simply do not resonate to them or accept them as truth anymore. Once free from those, you can connect the clear energy from one chakra to the other. By doing this you are opening a pathway to manifesting.

The timeframe of the pure energy that you are looking for – before other people's belief systems became your own – existed in a time right before you learned to read.

When you learned to read, you learned how to integrate, whether you realize it or not. In learning to read one first learns the alphabet as a basic foundation. Then you learn that every letter in the alphabet has a sound. Then you learn to your possible dismay that some letters have more than one sound.

114

Then based on the sounds of each individual letter, you learn that if you put more than one letter together you have the ability to form words. When you have the concept of words, you then learn that your mind must actually associate those words with something physical and tangible. And then you put them together to form a sentence. Then you learn the subsequent ability to create paragraphs from the individual words and sentences. When you put it all together, this learning becomes a way to communicate on a more sophisticated level.

You learn to take things even a step further when you learn to write. Your mind begins to understand and then expand enough to begin to integrate these concepts into your physical body. This learning integrates enough to not only to help you make a mental association, but then to enable you to take actual physical action with what you've learned, as in putting pen and words to paper.

Note that the process of learning to read is first taking place in the fifth and sixth chakras, the mind and communication chakras, rather than from the base or root chakra which is where the energy of money resides.

The reason we have the concept of the starving writer or starving artist is because this is where we see the ability of the energy to create, not connecting up with the energy of the upper chakras. In order to manifest we must connect up the balanced and clear energy of all of the chakras.

It is one thing to be able to read words and sentences and another to comprehend what you've read. And then it is quite another to then take what you've read and ostensibly comprehended and apply it in a real physical sense to your life.

Effective manifesting happens when you're fully using the energy of all of the chakras and then implementing that throughout your entire energy field.

Bobby

The gate to the entrance of the Fortuna residence was open and Bobby Dubois drove up the lane and parked his late model silver Mercedes at the arc of the circular drive. Obviously he was expected. He was pleased by the minimum of fuss needed to get in here. He liked things nice and easy. It helped with energy flow and that's what he was here for.

A massive fountain with an enormous figure of Zeus holding up the world stood in the center of the front yard. He wrinkled his nose in distaste. *How dreadful!* He obviously had his work cut out for him here.

He rang the bell exactly at the appointed hour. He prided himself on always being prompt. He was ever efficient. Time was money and he needed money since his nitwit of a boyfriend had gambled away nearly all of his inheritance. And now he had to work instead of sipping mai tais on a secluded beach somewhere with a pool boy attending to his every whim. *Unbelievable!* It was a bitter pill to swallow.

The door was answered by a very attractive well-groomed man whom Bobby instantly judged as probably gay. One did learn to pick up on these things. He thought it odd that Fortuna would have a gay man as a servant. He could have sworn the man was a homophobe.

"Bobby Dubois here."

"Yes, of course we're expecting you. Nice to meet you. I'm Brian Babcock, Nicholas' assistant."

Oh, so not a servant. This was getting better. The two exchanged a soft handshake as hazel eyes met clear green ones in instant and silent recognition.

"The maid was let go just this morning so I'm filling in with door answering duty until we get a replacement." Brian's full lips parted in a somewhat apologetic smile revealing small, even white teeth. "Nicholas isn't here yet."

"He's late." Bobby was somewhat irritated. Time was money.

"Yes, well, he should have been back by now. He just went out to grab a bite to eat."

Never patient with the act of waiting, Bobby said, "I'd like to get started while we wait. I just need to take a look around and take some notes and a few pictures and measurements."

Houses usually reflected those who lived in them, even on a subconscious level; and a cursory glance around told him this house didn't know what it wanted to be when it grew up.

Bobby pulled out his maps and compasses and other mysterious tools of Feng Shui wizardry from his elegant tote. As they moved from room to room Brian seemed stuck to him like glue. He wished he didn't find it necessary to hover. It interfered with his creative flow.

Even with this "Velcro" following him around, Bobby could immediately see exactly what some of the problems were regarding the fame issue. And one of those problems was a newly installed, gigantic sunken bathtub in the fame area of this house.

He imagined that one could have quite a party in there and become famous in his own unique way. He chuckled to himself in amusement. Beautiful and magnificent as the tub was, in business it signified "fame down the drain." It would be an expensive correction but it would have to go. Nicholas could well afford it. There wasn't a simple Feng Shui treatment in the world that would cure this one.

After two hours Bobby was almost through with his examinations. He bristled at the fact that Nicholas still hadn't even bothered to show up. The whole thing rubbed his fur the wrong way. What was he, chopped liver? He just didn't appreciate being treated as if he didn't exist. No one, not even the high and mighty Nicholas Fortuna, could treat him like he wasn't important. He had a means of dealing with situations like this. It was like his own little private Feng Shui cure and it worked perfectly for him.

He made his way into the kitchen on the premise of measuring something, Brian right behind him like a lingering five o'clock shadow.

"Don't you have something important to do?" Bobby said facetiously. It seemed lost on Brian. Bobby wanted to get rid of him for a few minutes. He wanted to check out the silverware. He didn't feel like explaining to Velcro Man that his interest in it didn't have anything to do with Feng Shui.

Money as Energy – Breaking Down the Barriers to Manifesting

Money is energy. So we need to learn how to work with that energy effectively and then do something positive with that. To begin, think of the energy of magnets. If you take two magnets and try to force their like poles together, there is absolutely nothing you can do to get them to stick together. They repel. A lot of people even subconsciously have this repellent energy when it comes to money. This energy, of course, is steeped in deep rooted fear based belief systems regarding money and self-worth.

It is helpful to try to identify where and when you began to equate your value/self-worth with money, which is pieces of paper. Figure out where that came from and why you really identify power with money. The truth is that it is the energy of money that has power, not the money itself.

Study why perhaps having an expensive car would make you feel like a million bucks. It is because somewhere you have this learned perception that money and things are power. They aren't. It's an illusion. In order for anything to happen that is forward moving in the money department, this illusion has to go.

Sure it's nice to have a nice car. But it's when you start tangling up the illusion with who you really are that the trouble starts. If you allow money and things to DEFINE who you are, then you're going to have some money challenges until you figure this all out. And that is because you've created negative polarity between your mind, body and spirit.

So if you do something simple like turn just one of the magnets around, you will find that they now stick together. Now we will learn how to do that, energetically speaking, with the energy of money. And then we will do something positive with it.

Money is energy. The real power comes from knowing how to work with the energy. Get to the root of the issue at a core level and you can make the issue transform and disappear.

So to begin the process of shifting polarities, let's create some money:

Saying that you don't have any money renders you completely powerless.

Go to the store and buy several sheets of green paper. Now take them home; and for as many times as you find yourself saying or thinking "I don't have any money," write "I don't have any money" on them. Do this for a month. Then cut them up into money size "bills." Now you have a big pile of green pieces of paper with words written on them. You have just created money or what looks like money. Now go try to use them to buy something. Is there any power there?

You can't use them to buy anything because they are completely worthless.

Do you begin to see how saying that you don't have any money renders you powerless? Do you begin to see there is no real power in "money?"

Now, if you could convince someone that your pieces of paper have value, then maybe you could use them as some form of exchange. But what is *written* on them, "I don't have any money," is completely negative in terms of perception of "value," therefore negating any possible "worth." Perceptions of value shape "reality."

So you see how easy it is to create something tangible with your thoughts, your intentions, and your actions.

In this example you have rendered your creation – something you created with your thoughts and action – and your ability to use what you created completely and totally without power. This is negative manifesting.

The Feng Shui Money Tree –
Something Out of Nothing

You now have a pile of green worthless paper. Or is it really worthless? If you perceive it to be worthless, then it is; and you can throw it away. However, perhaps there is something you can do with it that will help you in some way if you are willing to DO something.

Do you have any glue? Don't have any glue because you can't afford glue?

Do you have any flour? Don't have any flour because you don't have time or know how to bake?

Do you know anyone who would give you 1/2 a cup of flour? Or lend it to you?

Do you have any water? Don't have any water because you didn't pay your water bill? Is it raining where you are? Is there a perpetual puddle on your sidewalk? Is there residual water in your gutter? Do you get my point?

There are a million excuses why someone is unwilling to help themselves.

Now here is where alchemy comes in and it's pretty darn easy. **Here is how to transform energy:** Take the so-called worthless pieces of paper that you wrote, "I don't have any money" on and tear or crumple them up, put them in a large container and add some glue or make some glue out of flour and water. Or not. It's a choice.

Mix this all up with your hands and form the paper into a Feng Shui money tree that you place in the wealth corner of your home.

You have just created something positive out of your negative manifestations.

Do you really have to do this? No. I'm using it for illustrative purposes. However, it would be quite helpful to actually do it because you will be able to really feel the power of transformation take place. It is totally up to you. It's the difference between watching an exercise program and remarking how fit the host is or actually exercising along with it and becoming fit yourself.

"Do money trees really work?" You ask.

My answer: Do you believe they do? Whatever we ascribe power to is what has power. Maybe the paper money tree you made in and of itself has no power, but whatever you believe certainly does.

Does Feng Shui really work? Well, actually it does. There are a lot of people putting a lot of energy on this belief system and it has manifested into collective consciousness as truth. Whatever is fueled by energy has power.

My entire point here is about the energy of creation as it applies to manifesting. If you stop making excuses and give yourself the power to create something out of nothing, then there is power there.

The object of your creation doesn't necessarily have power, but the act of DOING begins to change things. You have opened your creative centers by DOING. And by being WILLING to do something with "nothing," you have taken your power back. You have aligned your will. You have created something. *This is what has the ability to propel you forward. This is called transformation.*

129

Lucky

Lucky finished her shift right after that handsome, arrogant movie star left. He was her last table. He had lingered around for no apparent reason and she couldn't wait to get out of here. How annoying. Yeah she knew who he was, but she wasn't going to give him the satisfaction of that. She was just tired of guys and their nonsense. All she wanted to do right now was make some money. Why did it seem so hard? Guys like that didn't know jack about how hard it was to make a living these days. Nor did they care. They were in their own little world – their own planet even.

She'd decided to treat herself and stay in a hotel for a few days while the fire inspectors did their thing. Even if she couldn't really afford it, she needed time to decompress; and there was no way she was going to stay with those crazy parents of hers. She couldn't handle the inevitable nightly drinking and arguing. She needed to be alone. It was a completely and totally shocking notion to realize she now had absolutely nothing that was worth anything. And one she couldn't even fully comprehend.

Fortunately, when she had returned from the conference the night before that imbecile had burned her house down, she'd left her suitcase in the car. The idiot had been too stoned to bring it in and she'd been too lazy to bring it in. So there it sat in her trunk for a day; and now she still had some clothes, however creased and crumpled. Thank God. Yes, it could have been worse. Maybe there was something to say for her luck after all.

The road to the hotel was narrow and twisty. As Lucky rounded a sharp curve she was suddenly startled by a gruesome sight. All she could say was, "Oh my God. Oh my God." There by the side of the road, semi-crunched and crumpled like origami against the guard rail was what was left of a dark green Jaguar. Hot steam was pouring out like a white geyser from its hood, or what was left of it. She pulled over as far as she could, got out of her vehicle and cautiously approached the twisted metal. The noxious odor of gasoline swirled acridly in her nostrils. She apprehensively peered inside and she could see someone. *Oh God! It was Him.* That famous guy. Nicholas Fortuna. Bright red blood was dripping down his chiseled face. At least that was still intact. Wasn't this her lucky day?

A pair of dark navy blue eyes met wide-eyed china blue ones in desperation. "Help me get out of here."

Working with the Energy of Money

You now know how to transform a negative into a positive. It isn't difficult. In fact it's easy if you realize your part in it and accept your ability to create. Along with that acceptance comes responsibility. In order to take responsibility you have to examine where your fears about money are. You cannot deal effectively with your money or anything you manifest if you are afraid of it. Why are you afraid of pieces of paper? Who told you that money is the definition of your self-worth?

The patterns and belief systems that were taught to you started your current issues with money. Now if you want to correct that, you first have to be *willing* to do so. Then you can begin to have a healthy relationship with money.

If we begin with a "poverty consciousness" – that is the belief that we do not have enough or that we aren't worthy to have enough – then this is part of the problem in manifesting money.

Believe that you have enough. Say, "I have everything I need." Even if you don't, this is how begin to manifest that you do. You're first setting an intention with your mind. If you say and believe that you really don't have everything you need, then that is what you are creating with your mind and the root chakra will simply follow suit.

Form follows thought. Thoughts have real energy. What you say and think becomes an ingrained belief system and therefore becomes true. If you believe you are limited because you don't have any money, then so it is. You have now limited yourself and your funds. If you believe that there are no limitations, then so it is.

And most importantly, you must be willing to take responsibility for what you create. This begins to align the will of the ego with universal will.

Debt and Financial Responsibility

The current financial markets are built on a fear based system. They react to every little nuance and utterance from anyone who is perceived to have power.

Along with this we've learned to become accepting of debt as a belief system and pattern. We believe in karma as debt. We believe in debt as an underlying and acceptable foundation. But the chakra systems and the truths of who we really are don't operate that way. So right there we have created disparity between mind, body, and spirit. And contrary to popular misconception, karma is not debt. It's more of a balance sheet.

What can you do about it? One of the areas that people seem to have trouble with is the actual management of money. You must be willing to take responsibility for the management of your money. Get smart about it. It isn't hard, particularly if you understand money as energy rather than pieces of paper that scare you or that appear to have dominion over you.

A lot of people got into trouble recently with negative amortization mortgages. And if you weren't paying attention, you suddenly owed much more than you started with.

If you didn't refinance perhaps you got into trouble. If you suddenly found yourself having trouble paying your bills, what did you do about it? Did you try to make a payment arrangement? Did you try to renegotiate your interest on your credit card bills? Did you try to change the billing dates on your cards to coincide with your payday? Did you try to consolidate your debt? Did you try to renegotiate your debt?

Or did you ignore all the money challenges, throw the never ending bills in the garbage, stop answering the phone and hope all the problems would just disappear? You must take responsibility for your money and the management of it, because the energy of money resides in the root chakra.

That is the chakra where creation begins. Taking responsibility helps to remove the fear and inertia that blocks the energy of creation. In not responding to and taking responsibility for what you have created, you render yourself powerless.

Get proactive. Learn. Figure out what you can do and then go do it. Doing this will help you remove the fear you have learned as a consequence of financial markets steeped in fear and other people's belief systems.

Lucky

"We should call 911."

"Fine, call them after you get me out of here. The car's going to blow up." He spoke a little too calmly. "Can't you smell that gasoline?"

Nicholas was right. The smell of gas was getting stronger. He had to get out now or he'd be blown to pieces. They both knew it.

Oh God! She didn't want anything to do with this. It was that damn bad luck again. Lucky didn't really know how she did it, but she somehow finally managed to free him from the twisted heap. Exhausted, scraped, scratched, and bleeding now herself, she dragged a limping and bloody Nicholas away from the mess that used to be his car. And then she called 911.

As they moved safely away from the wreck to the other side of the road, time seemed to be moving in slow motion. She felt as if she was in a bizarre tableau.

His breathing was shallow and she was worried that he might be in shock. She was trembling and panting from exertion. They were both a bloody mess. Good grief, she hoped he hadn't broken his neck or anything. She didn't want to get blamed for anything being wrong with this guy.

Even though they were expecting it, the loud and fiery explosion that soon followed startled both of them into each other's arms. Lucky thought to herself that she would hide there forever if she could. What was it with her and fire these days?

Manifesting 101

When trying to manifest anything, one must first make room and space for the new to come in. If you have a bunch of clutter and other papers lying around, how can anything new come in? Clear it all up. This frees up space for something new to enter. If it's pieces of paper that you desire to manifest, make room for them by getting rid of the paper that you no longer need and that no longer serves you.

Now, a lot of people think that manifesting has to do with praying, begging, pleading, and supplicating for what they want. It doesn't work that way. If you're doing that you are in your own way. Nothing can come in while you are still attached to the outcome. You have to let go and trust and believe that you have everything you need. If you are unable to do this, you are limiting the ability of the universe to assist you.

As an example, let's say you pray for money. That's fine. Now, while you're doing that you keep saying to yourself, "I don't know how this is going to happen, but I'm going to pray for it anyway." Ok, fine. Now instead

143

of going about your business, you keep focusing on how, how, how this is going to happen.

You worry. You fret. You think to yourself that "how" is an impossibility. Then nothing happens and you wonder why. This is when you lose your faith and your faith in your ability to create. You aren't creating. You are demanding. Then you are worrying. Then you, with your fear and doubt, are creating the very thing that you do not want. Nothing. Around and around this goes.

Here is another example: You pray, pray, pray for money. Again, you do not know how this will show up; but you remain open to it. Pretty soon a new opportunity opens up for you to be able to make more money – a new job, business venture, or similar.

You become so scared, intimidated and immobilized by the thought of having to make a change that you turn down the job or opportunity. You go back to praying for money, not understanding what just happened. You chose to turn down the opportunity. It was a choice. But you don't see it that way. You then lose your faith, and you sit there wondering why the universe won't save you.

Responsibility and Choices

In order to get yourself out of any situation you've created, you need to actually do something if you want to get out of it. You have to first take responsibility for all of your choices. Have no regrets. Accept the fact that you wouldn't have learned all the valuable things you've learned by making certain choices. Stop blaming circumstance, bad luck, or anyone else. This doesn't move you forward, but it keeps you stuck. You always have a choice even if you don't like the choice.

Stop making excuses. Go be a dishwasher if you have to while you are waiting for that pile of money that you believe will solve all your problems, to fall from the sky. There is nothing that should be "beneath" you when attempting to extricate yourself from your previous choices if that is what you truly desire to do. You are not stuck unless you truly believe you are. If you believe you are stuck, then you render yourself a powerless victim.

Here is what your linear mind is not seeing about being a dishwasher: While you are engaged in this job, one day a patron (or fellow dishwasher) starts choking. You save his life, and as a thank you he gives you a million dollars. You may be surprised that this person has an extra million to give away. Your linear mind sees something else. Try to be open to infinite possibilities. Otherwise you limit the universe's ability to work in your life. Limited thinking produces limited results.

Lucky and Nicholas

Hours later the paramedics, police, and fire department had come and gone. Nicholas had refused to go to the hospital. He was fine he said.

He fixed his deep, mysterious eyes on hers and said, "Take me home now."

It wasn't a request. The arrogance of the man was simply astounding.

"I was on my way to my hotel," She explained.

"You're a waitress who owns a hotel?"

"No, I don't own a hotel." She rolled her eyes in exasperation and her voice rose with fury. "I don't even have a house anymore!" She exclaimed in frustration.

She'd reached her limit for the day. Hot tears welled up in big blue eyes and began to spill over onto her blood stained peach colored cheeks.

He just stared at her, almost as if he'd just seen her for the very first time, mysterious pools of navy blue eyes seeming to bore a deep hole into her very soul. He brushed a silky strand of blond hair off her face.

"Take me home," he repeated. Softly this time. It was a request.

Green Lights

Here is an exercise in manifesting: This is not the same as manifesting a parking space with the help of a parking space angel.

You're driving on a road. You're in a hurry and worried about being late to wherever you're going. Try to remember that time is an illusion. Now manifest with your mind all green lights. How do we do this? Easy. Get a firm picture in your mind that you are already on time to wherever you are going.

"But there is so much traffic," you say.

Right there, let that go. It's in your way. Do not worry about the "how." You cannot manifest anything while you are trying to control the "how." Just know that you will get to where you are going on time and/or exactly when you are supposed to get there.

You do not tell the "stoplight fairies" how to make the lights all green. You just see them as green and you know they are green.

There is no doubt they are green. You do not worry about them turning red. They are green.

If you have an opportunity to change lanes into a lane where traffic is moving along nicely, then you do so without fear of being hit by another driver. You let go of the fear of being late. You just know you will be fine. And when the lights all start turning green, you actually DO have to step on the gas pedal and drive the car forward.

If you do catch a red light, you can use the power of that moment to study your inner dialogue and belief systems. Did you really believe you were able to manifest all green lights? Or did you believe it was impossible because the people in charge of such things like the timing of traffic control signals have made your attempts at manifesting all green completely impossible?

The Basic Principles of Manifesting

So, in manifesting, these are the basic principles:

1. You get a firm picture in your mind about what you think you desire. You visualize it as real in the physical realm.

2. You create it as three dimensional reality with your thoughts and intentions.

3. You stop worrying about "how," and "when."

4. You get completely out of the illusions.

5. You stop telling the universe what to do and how to make this show up for you.

6. When opportunity comes calling you let it in and perhaps even feed it some dinner.

7. You release your fears.

8. You detach, release, and completely let go of what you think you want. You then open to infinite possibilities, no matter what they look like at first.

9. You become WILLING to actually DO something about your situation, instead of making excuses.

Detach

Before we can release anything we must detach. Detachment is often mistaken for apathy. To detach does not mean that you do not care. It means that you and your ego-self are not attached to a certain outcome.

To detach means that instead of demanding you are at peace with whatever happens because you know it all is going to work out the way it's supposed to no matter what. It doesn't mean that you don't have an investment in something or someone. It means that you are willing to let go of what it is you think you want. This aligns your will with universal will.

Nothing can happen when you insist on being in control of the situation. Let go. Then the stuck energy or whatever it is you're holding onto comes to the surface and the whole thing then gets lifted up. Now you have opened a pathway for the universe to work its miracles and bring you what you desire.

Don't Give Up – Let Go and Release

Let's say that more than anything you want to manifest a relationship. (This could be anything – money included.) We will use balloon imagery as an example.

Whatever you are trying to manifest, intentions must first be set. Get a firm picture of your desires in your mind. Take a balloon and tether it to a string. Then fill it with helium and write the word "Relationship" on it or whatever it is that you think you want. Tie it securely to your ring finger and try to go about your day. You now have a "relationship." Now try to get dressed.

As part of manifesting, we must let go of things, rather than hold on to them too tightly. To do so hampers our progress. We must let go so that these things can fly as high as they need to.

Depending on your thought process patterns, you may expect that if you let go the balloon will return to you as a deflated piece of rubber. That is possible if you, (a) keep it tied to your finger for a long period of time and it loses its helium, and (b) fool yourself into thinking you are releasing it as you release it into the confined space of a particular room in your house.

However, also depending on your thought process, you may know that once you let it go where it needs to go, say up to the heavens, it returns in a different form, and probably not as a deflated piece of rubber that hits you in the face on its way back to you.

So now you have a choice between the need to control and trust in the transformation process. Where is your balloon?

There is an option to give up on the balloon ever flying high and transforming, which most people opt for when they figure out that the balloon isn't going anywhere if it's tied to their finger. But what most people refuse to face in this situation is that if they just let go they could have what they desire.

So they give up, which essentially equates to having a tantrum. This doesn't do anything whatsoever to assist in the transformation process.

154

In this instance you are in your own way. In this instance what you think you want and your need to control is keeping you from getting what you desire. You have to let go in order for transformation to occur.

To hang on limits the way this returns to you. You don't want it to return as a balloon, do you? You want what you *wrote* on the balloon to manifest.

Before you let it go, it is just what it is – a thought, a desire, written on something you are attached to. It is by letting it go and giving it freedom to fly that you give it the opportunity to transform.

Once you do let go completely, do not be attached to the outcome. Do not go flying around looking for the balloon. Do not try to follow the balloon into the sky or attempt to control where it goes. Do not give the balloon instructions on how to get where it is going or what it is supposed to do when it gets there.

Allow whatever you have manifested – put forth in thought, word, and action – to come back to you, not as a flat one or two-dimensional concept but as true form.

155

Lucky

Lucky never made it to "her" hotel. After she'd taken Nicholas home as he'd commanded on that crazy fateful day of the accident, she'd stayed in his guesthouse on the beach. He'd insisted, saying she'd saved his life and it was the least he could do. He was grateful.

"No sense staying in a hotel if you don't own it." He'd grinned that amazing grin and the smile lit up his blue eyes. She'd stayed.

Carla

Carlos' information had devastated Carla. But she already knew it. The five of pentacles had repeatedly shown up in her tarot card readings the last few weeks. It was the card of adversity. *Penalidad*. The cards were one thing that never failed her.

When he'd first told her the news she was stunned. *"¿Podria repetir, por favor? It cannot be true!"* All of their dreams rested on those pieces of paper that made up that one all important test, the Bar Exam. And of course the paper that would follow. Money. *Dinero*. Then she'd flung things at him – anything she could get her hands on – like an enraged and wounded animal, wildly screaming obscenities at the top of her lungs in Spanish and English. They had become citizens! He had finished law school! Everything they had worked for and now all their plans were ruined! *Idiot!* Eventually he'd fled.

"Where are you going?" She managed through clenched and barred teeth. She had run out of things to hurl through the air.

He hung his head as if he were a very bad dog. "I'm going to buy some lottery tickets, my love. Then I'm going to the race track. If you were really any good with those damn tarot cards you could produce the winning numbers and horses!" He slammed the door on the way out.

Carla left too. She couldn't bear to look at the mess she'd made during her tirade. Her colorful clothing was scattered all around the house from her childish fit of rage, since she had ripped it all out of the closets and drawers. Pieces of broken china were everywhere she looked. There was no sense in being in this house if they were going to lose it. She knew she was getting ahead of herself. She knew she was being irrational, but she couldn't even bear the thought. She loved this house. It was everything to her.

Their child, Eduardo, was in pre-school and wasn't due to be picked up until later in the afternoon. She had time to collect herself. She pocketed her precious tarot cards. Maybe the cards would speak to her and tell her what she wanted to hear.

Carla backed her little black sports car out of the garage and headed toward the beach. She needed to think. She felt shattered and confused. Her friend Juanita had once shown her a quiet and peaceful place. It was private. Maybe she could clear her head there. She did not understand the universe. *At all.*

Carla parked the car, got out, and made her way a short distance to an obscure opening through the trees. If one didn't know this was here, one would never see it. It wasn't overtly visible from the street. She only knew because Juanita had shown her one day and she'd filed the information away in her memory for safekeeping.

The wind parted the trees, as if to welcome her, and revealed a set of concrete stairs that led down to the beach. There were at least four hundred of them, maybe five hundred. Undaunted and still full of adrenaline she began the descent, not worrying for now about the climb back up.

When she reached the bottom, she removed her shoes and let the warm sand caress her soft bare feet. It felt like total freedom. She walked down to the water's edge and let the frothy surf come up to meet her ankles in a cold, wet kiss. It was better than no kiss at all. She soaked it in. It was a crisp sunny day. She saw one lone surfer out in the waves and no one else. Good. This was her own private beach for now. She was entitled.

She walked for a bit and settled into a secluded area near where the trees first met the sand. There was a cute little house close by, maybe a guesthouse she surmised, with a large estate adjacent. As she settled into her spot, Carla closed her eyes and let her mind go into peaceful daydreaming. She imagined what it would be like to live in this place where the sand met the sea. What heaven it would be to listen to the ocean sing its lullaby every single night. She wondered if the people that lived here were grateful for that or if the music of the sea eventually became so ordinary for them that they didn't hear it anymore.

Her brows knit into a frown. There was no way she was going to lose her house. Carlos would just have to think of something!

Carla opened her eyes. The surfer was out of the water and was coming toward her. He was waving and gesturing frantically with one arm while the surfboard was neatly tucked under the other. The wetsuit clung like a second skin to his toned physique. She wondered what the problem could be. He seemed to be limping and he was walking straight toward her. *How irritation!* She just wanted to be alone! And she had every right to that.

He stopped and stood three feet in front of her, pointing his finger at her. "You!" Do you want to go to jail?"

Carla stared at him, a stunned mute.

"What?" she finally managed.

"I said, do you want to go to jail?"

Being Grateful

It may seem as if you have absolutely nothing to be grateful for. If you believe that, you keep yourself as a victim, thus rendering yourself powerless to create and manifest. Nothing can return to you while you insist on remaining in the space of ungratefulness.

Every day should start with being grateful whether you feel like that or not, because it successfully opens up pathways to receiving. Find one single thing in your life that you are grateful for, whether it be a simple meal or even just your breath. These are gifts.

Gratefulness comes from the heart chakra. It is unconditional love for your life, for your breath, for everything that occurs in your life, "good" or "bad." It's like yin and yang.

When the heart chakra is open, the manifesting energy that flows up from the chakras below it can meet with the heart energy. This is how the "base of the matter" gets shifted, thus transforming into a higher, more pure form of energy that can go out and then circulate back to you. It's a flow. What stands in the way of being grateful is your distortion of the illusion of the way you think things are.

Being grateful, even briefly has the effect of moving you out of your patterns, illusions, and belief systems and opens a pathway for abundance of all sorts to return to you easily and effortlessly.

Judgments

You cannot be grateful and judgmental and controlling at the same time. You cannot serve two masters.

When you're judging something, you're judging it from your own frame of reference and perspective. You are judging it from the "I" part of yourself. Judgment stands in the way of being grateful and not being grateful stands in the way of having energy flow. Blocked energy flow stands in the way of manifesting. Let go of judgments, illusions, patterns and belief systems that block the path to manifesting.

166

Forgiveness

It is difficult to effectively manifest when we are blaming others for our circumstances. We must forgive. Forgiveness must come from both the linear mind and the spirit. You may think that you've forgiven already; but if you've only done so in the physical realm, the process isn't complete.

To forgive completely, go into a relaxed or meditative state of mind. Call to you the person's spirit that you wish to forgive. See the person coming toward you. Establish a flow from your heart chakra to theirs. If this is not possible, just send them forgiveness energy from your heart chakra. At the same time, with your mind, state your intention to forgive.

There is one more thing to do, even if you do not understand it. Thank them for teaching you a lesson in love, bless them, and then release them. Then see what happens. Forgiving in this manner frees up previously blocked energy that you can then use for manifesting.

Carla

"Hired help is not allowed on this beach!" The man was fuming.

Carla had never been so insulted in her life. She was not hired help! What was he talking about? She felt the blood rush up to her cheeks as the shame of who she used to be caught in her throat like an old chicken bone. Certainly she did not look like that wild gypsy anymore. How could he mistake her for someone's servant? She was Carla Ortega, the wife of an *abagado*. Well, an almost lawyer.

Her brow furrowed in consternation. "I am not hired help, Senor. I am . . ."

"I don't care who you are. You don't live here and you're in my backyard. You're trespassing. We pay millions of dollars for this view and you're blocking it. Now get out of here before I call the police."

He had a right to keep the riffraff off of his beach. Besides he didn't need anyone, even a maid, seeing him struggle out there in the waves.

Carla felt like someone had cut her off at the knees and turned to flee from this very rude person before her legs gave out. She wouldn't be able to climb all those stairs with legs of rubber. As she turned to go, a lone tarot card flew out of her pocket as if it had wings and landed face up right in front of Nicholas' bare toes on the sandy ground. It was the Page of Cups. Reversed.

All Carla wanted to do was run away as fast as she could. But the tarot cards had stopped her now. Even if her legs weren't made of *rubberish*, it was a sign. She had a spiritual duty. She knew she was exactly where she was supposed to be.

Carla knew the card well. The picture on it was of a young man standing alone at the seashore holding a cup. Inside the cup is a fish that pops its head out unexpectedly and delivers a message of inspiration to the self-absorbed man. Carla was willing to be the fish. But she didn't have to be nice about it, did she?

Tersely, she began. "Senor, apparently I have a message for you whether either of us likes it or not."

170

A look of puzzled disbelief crossed his face as he watched her pick the card up from the sand. The woman was obviously insane. But there was something compelling and magnetic about her. He didn't know exactly why, but he nodded his head in agreement and let her continue.

Carla gulped and went on. She could tell he thought she was *loco*. And she didn't want to go to jail.

"You now will have opportunity for new and different ways of learning. These opportunities can lead you to great joy. You will find new and unexpected ways to express your emotions and creativity. This is time for a new beginning, new relationship, or new perspectives on old ways of doing things. It is the beginning of a spiritual journey." She paused and took a very deep breath.

"Now, you must choose a sea shell, make a wish from the heart and cast it out on the water. It will soon return to you in a different form with all of your answers." *Transformation*.

With that she shyly and hesitantly took his hand and led him closer to the water. To her amazement he didn't pull back. He came along willingly. She watched him bend over, carefully choose a shell, concentrate on it as if his life depended on it, and cast it out to sea. Carla followed suit. She knew the message was for her too.

Epilogue

Lucky was lucky enough from her association with Nicholas to see that being rich and famous did not necessarily bring happiness. She no longer cared if she ever became either. Once she let go of that attachment to outcome, her life began to unfold in magical ways. She took up yoga and meditation and even convinced Nicholas to join her.

She went to Elayne's ex-husband for chiropractic adjustments and was able to work more hours at the diner. She eventually dug herself out of debt and made peace with her parents. She learned to accept them just the way they were. And she began to see that even with all of their flaws they had given her many opportunities in life, for which she was grateful. She thanked them and stopped blaming them.

She stayed in the guesthouse for a while and focused on her dream of writing. Soon that dream became reality and she wrote many magazine articles for Elayne's magazine. Today, Lucky would tell you that her luck had definitely changed. She is putting the finishing touches on her novel. Of course she and Nicholas eventually ended up together. They were soul mates.

Elayne helped Nicholas recover fully from his accident by teaching him gentle yoga. She too began to realize that money did not necessarily bring happiness. Through counseling, acupuncture, self-healing techniques, meditating, and balancing her chakras, she was able to let go of her fears, victim role, and poverty consciousness.

Bobby's Feng Shui cures began to work and soon Elayne's warm and positive energy began to attract more and more students. She was able to get her magazine just as slick as could be. She sold many subscriptions, lots of advertising and even made some yoga videos. She wrote a vegetarian cookbook which sold millions of copies. She met a very handsome African American man at her studio and they began an exclusive relationship. They are now happily married with two children. And even though she is eco-conscious, she no longer saves used aluminum foil.

Carla agreed to be Nicholas' maid for a short period of time while Carlos restudied for the bar exam. Carlos did not win the lottery. He passed the exam and got re-hired. They eventually were able to buy a house on the beach where Carla is grateful for the music of the ocean every single day. She gives tarot card readings once a week at Elayne's yoga studio just because she loves to do so. Her metaphysical store will soon be open. It's right next to Elayne's studio.

Bobby continued to do Feng Shui and began to derive great satisfaction from the transformations he was able to effect. He broke up with his boyfriend and started dating Brian. Brian made him return Nicholas' silverware.

And Nicholas? He's a work in progress.

Other Products Available By This Author

Voice of the Angels – A Healing Journey
Spiritual Cards
by Dyan Garris

The Journal

A beautiful thirty card deck based on scenes from the guided fantasy *A Healing Journey*. Each card has its own special channeled message in rhythmic quatrain verse from the angels. The box of cards includes a 67 page instruction booklet showing twelve ways to lay out the cards, *Transformational Healing Exercise*, healing affirmations, and more. These cards were not computer generated and therefore have different core energy than similar decks. Real crystals and other elements were used to create the cards. A journal is available separately. Use for spiritual growth, divination and spiritual transformation.

Voice of the Angels Cookbook
Talk To Your Food! – Intuitive Cooking
by Dyan Garris

This is an adventure in opening the creative centers and communicating with your food so that it can transform from raw ingredients into what truly nourishes you on every level. The book includes twelve food related channeled messages, several "Intuitively Speaking" paragraphs which explain how to prepare the recipe using one's own unique creativity, and sixty full color photographs.

CDs by Dyan Garris

There are six CDs in the series of music and meditation for healing, relaxation, guided meditation, chakra balance, help in sleeping, and vibrational attunement. Each CD consists of six or seven tracks of instrumental music plus a guided meditation on the last track. Titles are: *A Healing Journey – The Voice of the Angels, Moment by Moment – Music For The Soul, Reflection, Patterns, Illusions,* and *Connections.* Each CD vibrates to a specific chakra and each is for a specific purpose.

There are four compilation CDs – two volumes of music only and two volumes of guided meditation only. Music only compilation titles are: *Spiritus Sanctus*, Volume 1 and 2. Guided meditation only compilation titles are: *Perfect Pathways*, Volume 1 and 2.

The CD *Release* is eleven tracks of soothing instrumental relaxation music for those who need a release. The very angelic vocals of award winning recording artist Amber Norgaard can be heard on the songs "Breathe" and "Sleep."

Voice of the Angels Meditation Basket

Meditation Basket

The Meditation Basket includes all six soul soothing CDs in the series of music and guided meditation for self-healing, chakra balancing, relaxation and vibrational attunement by Dyan Garris. The beautiful lined reusable basket comes with an angelic scroll of healing affirmations, authentic and powerful Tibetan meditation crystal, high quality incense and holder, and a clean burning, great smelling Reiki charged meditation candle in its own jar with its own affirmation. Beginner to experienced will find the "Journeys" on the last track of each CD healing and refreshing!

The Meditation Journal

Voice of the Angels Meditation Journal is for recording your meditative journeys. It is designed to be used with the CD series of music and guided meditation by Dyan Garris for self-healing, chakra balance, stress release, help in sleeping, and vibrational attunement of mind, body, and spirit. However, it can be used for recording any meditation journey or nightly dreams. Transformation and deeper levels of learning can be achieved by keeping a record of what transpires in a meditative state. *The Meditation Journal* serves as a helpful and integrative tool between the linear mind and the subconscious, meditative mind.

About The Author
Dyan Garris

Dyan Garris has helped many people move forward in their lives with her gifts of clairvoyance, clairaudience, and clairsentience. Dyan is also a voice recognition psychic and trance channel. Dyan became aware of her gifts at a young age and spent years learning how to use these gifts to help others.

In 2005 she created a CD series of instrumental music and meditation for self-healing, chakra balance, relaxation, and vibrational attunement of mind, body, and spirit. Each CD vibrates to a specific chakra and contains several tracks of music plus a guided meditation at the end. Ms. Garris' music can be heard on numerous radio stations, nationally as well as internationally.

Dyan is the author, developer and artist of *Voice of the Angels – A Healing Journey Spiritual Cards, Voice of the Angels – Talk To Your Food! Intuitive Cooking, The Book of Daily Channeled Messages* and *Fish Tale of Woe – Lost at Sea*. She also writes the *Daily Channeled Message*, which posts on her website www.voiceoftheangels.com

For further information visit: www.newagecd.com, www.dyangarris.com and www.myspace.com/voiceoftheangels.